Jerry Flemmons'
MORE
TEXAS
SIFTINGS

Jerry Flemmons'
MORE TEXAS SIFTINGS

ANOTHER
BOLD AND
UNCOMMON
CELEBRATION
OF THE LONE
STAR STATE
★

TEXAS CHRISTIAN UNIVERSITY PRESS ★ FORT WORTH

Acknowledgments

Original *Fort Worth Star-Telegram* illustrations and design by
Don Cook, Dean Eubank, Bronc Sears, Bob Davis, and Drew White.

Computer documentation transfer by Mike Gerst.

Book & cover design by Margie Adkins Graphic Design.

Entries are for the most part in their original form. In a few instances, slight editing has been done for the reader's convenience.

Library of Congress Cataloging—in—Publication Data

Flemmons, Jerry.
Jerry Flemmons' more Texas Siftings : another bold and uncommon
celebration of the Lone Star State by Jerry Flemmons
p. cm.
ISBN 0-87565-179-8
1. Texas--Miscellanea. I. Title
F386.5.F57 1997
976.4 -- dc21   97-26829
                                                          CIP

CONTENTS

Alexander Sweet's original *Texas Siftings*, circa 1881.

*Texans ignore 'better,'
long ago forgot the
useless word 'good.'
Everything in Texas is 'best.'*

Edward Smith, *Account of a Journey
Through North-Eastern Texas*, 1849

LIFE IN THE WILDERNESS

I remember, upon one occasion, after riding all day through a dense forest region in Northwestern Texas, in the winter of 1850-1, without the slightest indication of a road or even trail to guide me, and during a severe storm of snow and rain, and without having met with a single human being during the entire day, that I suddenly came out into a small clearing in the center of which was a very diminutive log cabin, from which arose a cheerful smoke, indicating the presence of occupants. . . I therefore gladly turned my jaded horse toward the hut, and, on my approach, a woman, some half a dozen children, and about as many dogs emerged there from. . . I begged to inquire if I could be accommodated with lodgings for the night, to which the woman very obligingly replied, "Wall, now, stranger, my ole man he ar out on a bar track, but I sort-o-reckon maybe you mought git to stay," [and after dinner] I lighted my pipe, seating myself before a cheerful log fire, for the first time since my arrival took a survey of the establishment.

It consisted of one room about fourteen feet square, with the intervals between the logs not chinked, and wide enough in places to allow the dogs to pass in and out at their pleasure. There was an opening for the door, which was closed with a greasy old beef's hide, but there were no windows, and no floor excepting the native earth.

The household furniture consisted of two small benches of the most primitive construction imaginable, and two bedsteads, each made by driving four forked stakes into the ground, across which poles were placed, and then covered transversely by flour-barrel staves, the whole structure surmounted by a sack of prairie hay, upon which I observed the remains of an antiquated coverlid that had evidently seen much service.

The table furniture consisted of one tin milk-pan, three tin cups, two knives and three forks, two of the latter having but one prong each. The tout ensemble gave every indication of the most abject destitution and poverty; indeed, the hostess informed me that she had not, previous to my arrival, tasted sugar, tea, or coffee for three months; yet, as strange as it may appear, she seemed contented with her situation, and considered herself about as well to do in the world as most of her neighbors. . .

Before I left the house my hostess inquired of me If I knew how to write; and, upon learning that my education had extended that far, she desired me to act as her amanuensis, while she dictated a letter to a friend, "way down in ole Massasip [Mississippi]." Having a pencil and some old letters in my pocket, I told her I would take down what she desired to communicate, copy it in ink on my return to the fort, and send it for her through the post, which seemed to give her great pleasure, whereupon I seated myself, and asked her what she wished me to write. She said:

"Tell um, stranger, thar's narry fever-n'agur down this-a-way. . . Tell um, stranger, Davy he raised a powerful heap o' corn and taters this year. . . Tell um, stranger, thar's a mighty smart chance o'varmints in these yere diggins."

And thus she went on throughout the entire letter, which she "'lowed was a peart hand write." I translated it literally in her own words on my return home, and forwarded it to its destination in Mississippi, and I sincerely hope the good woman has received an answer ere this.

Randolph B. Marcy,
Thirty Years of Army Life on the Border, 1866

SAM BASS HITS A FEW STAGECOACHES

On his return from San Antonio to Cove Hollow, on or about the 20th of December, 1877, Sam Bass and his gang conceived the plan of robbing the stage running from Fort Worth to Cleburne, Texas. They took their positions on the roadside, about ten miles from Fort Worth, and awaited the approach of the stage, which reached that point late in the evening, bearing two passengers. They threw their guns on the driver and ordered him to throw up his "props" [slang for "hands"], which he did promptly. They then called to the passengers to come forth and hold up their hands, while Bass examined their finances. The others held their guns on the victims, while Sam proceeded very coolly through their pockets. The results of his search was only eleven dollars. After some complaint about the meager state of the purses, and giving it as their opinion that there ought to be a law to prohibit such poor trash from traveling on the highway. . .

. . .[A]bout the middle of February [Bass decided to rob] the stage running between Fort Worth and Weatherford. Passing the former place, they proceeded to look for a suitable spot for their operations, which they found at a gulch near Mary's Creek, about midway between Marysville and Fort Worth. They tied their horses, and masking themselves, they laid in wait by the roadside. In due time the stage came up, having on board three passengers. They presented their guns on the driver, saying they wanted some money. Bass called for the passengers to step out, which was promptly obeyed. No resistance was offered, and Bass went through them as usual, getting about $70 in money and three watches.

This gave Bass considerable encouragement. He remarked, with evident satisfaction, "Well, this is the best haul I ever made out of a stage, and I've tapped nine of 'em so far. There's mighty poor pay in stages, generally, though."

Authentic History of Sam Bass and His Gang, printed in the Monitor Book and Job Printing Establishment, Denton, Texas, 1878

★ ★ ★ ★ ★ ★ ★ ★ ★ ★ ★ ★ ★ ★ ★ ★ ★

COWBOYS GO ON STRIKE

We, the undersigned cowboys of Canadian River, do these presents agree to bind ourselves into the following obligations, viz:

First: That we will not work for less than $50 per mo. and we further more agree no one shall work for less than $50 per mo. after the 31st of Mch.

Second: Good cooks shall also receive $50 per mo.

Third: Any one running an outfit [foreman] shall not work for less than $75 per mo.

Any one violating the above obligations shall suffer the consequences. Those not having funds to pay board after March 31 will be provided for 30 days at Tascosa.

1883 strike notice filed in the Texas Panhandle, signed by 24 cowboys; the strike against the Panhandle Cattlemen's Association, which fixed cowboy salaries at $25/$30 monthly, failed, and the striking 24 cowboys were blacklisted

OLD—VERY—OLD JOKE

A lady from the East who was visiting Texas for the first time noticed some animals that had been freshly branded and she exclaimed, "Look at those monogrammed cattle!"

STAMPEDE: A SYMPHONY OF SCATTERING STEERS

You may attempt to picture in your mind what a stampede of several thousand longhorn cattle is like, but one can't visualize the actual scene. I shall attempt to draw a mental picture of what the old rawhide viewed and contended with during a cattle run. . . .

Many things can scare a herd. For instance, a wolf which runs into a herd to pull down a calf or something that may startle just one animal; the fear caused to the one animal will spread through the whole herd instantly. While a herd is on their own ground it is not so easily scared, but when bedded off their home range, for instance, when on a drive, the herd is prone to stampede over trifles. . .

The herd may be bedded and arise instantly. Looking at a herd arising appears as if the earth is heaving up with an accompanying roar, a swish like sound, and the clashing of horns. While the cattle are running, the pounding of their feet on the earth sounds as the roll of many muffled drums. The clashing of the horns gives off a sound similar to that of many muffled cymbals. The two sounds is quite a symphony, but broken by the discordant yell of the waddies trying to divert the herd's attention and put the animals to milling. What I mean by milling is to start the cattle to running in a circle, instead of straight away.

If the herd was not scared too badly and not running too fast, the critters will follow their leaders. Our job was to force the leading critters from their straight course. That was performed by riding at the side and to the front of the leading animals and crowding the critters.

Most of the time we could accomplish our purpose in stopping a run, but occasionally we would fail. If we failed the cattle would be scattered hither and yond.

Suppose it was dark and storming while a stampede was in progress, which it often was. Then imagine, if you can, riding at the head of several thousand wild, frightened and running cattle, and while riding, crowding your mount against the running cattle trying to force the animals off their course. Suppose your horse stumbled and threw you in front of the running cattle? Of course, the result of such event is obvious. Talk about daring riders, that was one position the word daring does not express strong enough.

Sand in your gizzard, as the cowhand use to say, expresses such riders more accurately.

The Library of Congress, WPA Writers Project; from interview with cowboy/rancher A.M. Garrett of Fort Worth, age 83; undated, but about 1934
Traditional

★ ★ ★ ★ ★ ★ ★ ★ ★ ★ ★ ★ ★ ★ ★ ★

TEXAS: A WORLD UNTO ITSELF

It takes half an hour to drive from PITTSBURG to OMAHA, and it is only 54 miles from BOSTON to DETROIT, but the POINT-BLANK route from EARTH to PARADISE is via GASOLINE. There are COLFAX. If you try your VERIBEST, you can find UTOPIA. Texas towns all, and while Massachusetts has one Boston, Texas has BOSTON, NEW BOSTON and OLD BOSTON. No Harvard and no beans, but PRINCETON and OKRA.

Without leaving Texas, you can go to Holland, Malta, India, China, Ireland, Italy, Trinidad, Turkey, Palestine, Scotland, Egypt, Erin and Moravia.

You can visit Jericho, Liverpool, London, Macedonia, Moscow, Manchester, Tampico, Tokio, Troy, Vienna, Warsaw, Tunis, Odessa, Newcastle, Paris, Petersburg, Rugby, Sparta, Sheffield, Stockholm, Athens, Bolivar, Cadiz, Canton, Dorchester, Dresden, Dublin, Edinburg, Geneva, Genoa, Oxford and Bogata.

These are all cities, towns or villages in Texas. Named after more famous cities? Not so. Take Dublin, for instance. In the early days a large double cabin was built where the villagers sought refuge during Indian raids. They "doubled in" to "Double Inn" at such times and the town was eventually named Dublin. . .

You will find Blackfoot & Bluetown, Dial & Telephone, Alto & Tennerville, Dresden & China, Cash & Price. There are Cement & Friendship, Commerce & Industry, Concord & Grapevine, Concrete & Stonewall, Energy & Pep, Mickey & Finney, Paris & Green, Sherwood & Forest, Burlington & Rock Island.

There are Desoto & Dodge. . . Wells & Fargo, Fisk & Goodrich, Hope & Crosby, Morgan & Vanderbilt. Oilso, you will find Humble and Oiltown, Texico & Gasoline, Phillips & Petroleum. . .

There is mixed company in Booth & Lincoln, Burns & Allen, George & Washington, Carmen & Mirando City, Happy & Chandeler, Cordele & Hull, Davey & Jonesboro, Elsa & Maxwell, Irene & Dunn, Lillian & Russell, James & Monroe, Ogden & Nash, Fred & Waring. You will also find Franklin, James, Elliott & Roosevelt. . .

Texas is the place where:
   Folks undress in PLAINVIEW
   Take baths on FRIDAY in COLOGNE
   Get PETTY in the CACTUS at the CROSS ROADS
   Where girls have a STRUCTURE as STOUT as VENUS
   And are CONTENT to seek COMFORT with TARZAN.
They are Texas towns.

John Randolph, *Texas Brags*, 1951

"I AM GOING TO TELL YOU OF ONE NIGHT WHEN WE HAD A STAMPEDE WHICH I CAN'T FORGET. . ."

The day had been a hot one and hard one on the critters. The animals didn't do much grazing until about an hour before sunset and them continued to graze past their usual bedding time, which was around dusk. This night a heavy cloud showed suddenly in the North and came on fast. A heavy rain with sky-fire came on. The sky-fire was scaring the critters causing all of us to do plenty of riding in order to hold the animals from going on a run.

Suddenly, hail about the size of pigeon eggs began to fall. When the hail hit the critters they decided to go somewhere in spite of hell, highwater of rawhides, and the animals did that pronto.

While working in that hail storm was one time I found the ten gallon honk [head] cover a mighty handy article. If we rawhides had been wearing any ordinary hat, the hail stones would have knocked us loco. Our heads were saved, but the rest of our bodies was full of welts from the pounding of the hail stones. Our hosses were loco from being pelted and we could hardly control the poor devils. About half of the mounts started pitching. Those which were not pitching, were running away from their riders. We were lucky that the cattle and hosses all were going with the storm. In addition to loco hosses, critters and half loco rawhides, it was dark and we couldn't see what we were running into.

The hail pelted us for about ten minutes or so, but that was more than enough and when the hail stopped no one could reckon where the other riders were or what became of the herd.

Us waddies lit out to find the herd soon as the hail ceased falling. The herd started towards the Colorado River and we all reckoned the same way, and that was it was still traveling in that direction. We knew that when the herd reached the river it would have to stop or swim the river. From where the herd started was about ten miles from the river. In face of the fact that we all were separated, we had reckoned the same way and were heading for the Colorado. Soon as the hail stopped we all began to shoot our guns to let each other know where each other were and it was not long till all of us had our bearings. Most of us had reached the herd just before it reached the river. We just let the [herd] run until it reached the river and there, of course, it stopped, and the animals went to milling and we went to work keeping the critters from scattering. We finally got the herd quieted and settled, then started the herd back.

The Library of Congress, WPA Writers Project; interview with Albert Erwin of Fort Worth, age 88, 1938

ON THE NIGHT OF MARCH 13, 1912, TRAIN NO. 9, OF THE SOUTHERN PACIFIC, RUNNING BETWEEN EL PASO AND SAN ANTONIO, WAS HELD UP BY TWO ROBBERS, WHICH RAIL CLERK DAVID ANDREW TROUSDALE KILLED (RATHER BLOODILY, TOO)

One of the men got on the engine at Dryden, although I did not know this until the train came to a stop out on the railroad line. But a minute or two thereafter the negro porter came to the door of the car and called me. I recognized his voice. Just about then I was finishing up my work before reaching Sanderson. The negro porter said, "They's some robbers out here." As I opened the door, I looked down the barrel of a gun one of the robbers was holding on me. . .

Well, the big fellow went into the cars and the other remained on the outside. In the mail car he got hold of five pouches and one of these was cut open, the man seeing some registered letters, threw these back into the pouch with the intention of getting them later on.

There was only two express packages removed. One of these was valued at $2 and the other at $35. So you see there was not a great deal obtained by the robber who was doing the work.

But you know the fellow was making me madder all the time. If I was not holding my hands high enough he seemed to take delight in jabbing me in the side with his gun. However, I kept jollying him along [and] wondered how to kill him. I was mad for I was determined I would have it out with him for jabbing me in the side and bruising me up. I'd have fought him with my fists had it come to that.

Well, I saw a maul lying on top of the barrels of oysters. These mauls are built something like a croquet mallet, only the handle is about as thick as the handle of a hatchet. . . You know you can hit an awful blow with such a maul. Why, I've broken up a box of ice at a blow. . . He was stooped over looking at packages. . . I lifted the maul from the top of the oyster barrel. . . I struck him at the base of the skull. The first blow broke the man's neck. . . I struck him a second and a third time. . . After that, I saw that he was done for [and] took the man's Winchester.

I decided to fire a shot through the roof of the car to attract attention. . . I soon heard the other robber on the outside of the car talking low. . . Pretty soon I saw a head poked out from back of some baggage. . . I saw his head again and I cut down on him. The bullet struck him about an inch above the left eye. It passed through his skull and then passed out through the car.

David Trousdale's account of the attempted train robbery, reported in the *San Antonio Express*, March 15, 1912; the slain robbers were Ben Kilpatrick and Ed Welch, two recently paroled convicts

★ ★ ★ ★ ★ ★ ★ ★ ★ ★ ★ ★ ★ ★ ★ ★ ★ ★

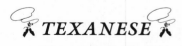

TEXANESE

Fencelifter

Said of a sudden torrential rain so strong the runoff water washed out—"lifted"—fences. Such rains also were called "gullywashers" and "frogstranglers."

FORT WORTH IN 1884

We stayed in Fort Worth a few days. This was grand after having been on the road about four weeks. Fort Worth was really a boom town [with] a new rail road, street shows of every description and people of every kind, cattlemen, horse traders, bone haulers, gamblers and fakers of every conceivable nature.

The town at night resembled some noted seashore pavilion. The streets and sidewalks were jammed. There were amusements of almost every description and everywhere. It seemed that every other door on either side was aglow and the music was mostly from fiddles and organs. There were not many violinists but many fiddlers, dance halls, saloons, shooting galleries and on the street, soap box orators and an occasional street preacher.

During the day, it was horse trading, cattle selling and conversations which usually included where was the best place to locate or where are you from and to what part of the state are you going.

There were big herds of cattle from the west, for this was a big shipping point. Men with four to six horse wagons loaded with bones, others with horns and still others with only cowhides for sale. Many of the hides were so green or fresh, one could whiff the odor from them for several blocks. One might wonder where so many bones hides and horns could have been collected.

If you could have made a trip across Western Texas during early spring at that time, you could have easily seen. As cattle wintered themselves on the dried grass, they were always poor by spring and as soon as the new grass began shooting up they would quit eating the dried grass and [with] the difficulty of trying to get enough of the young, tender green grass, they lost flesh and many of them would become so poor and weak, they would find themselves too weak to rise and after a few days would die of hunger.

At this time, one riding over the country would scarcely ever be out of sight of a carcass. . . Cowhides sold at about $1.00 per hide. Many people made their living by riding the distant range and skinning dead cattle for their hides and no doubt in many instances, where it was seen that the cow could not regain her strength, she was killed and skinned and nothing further said about the matter.

J.F. Harrell, describing a visit
to Fort Worth in an
unpublished manuscript,
written about 1964

HOW TO ORDER GRUB THE WAY YOU WANT IT

Rocking Chair Ranche Limd.
Aberdeen,
Collingsworth Co.,
Texas
May 31st 1892

Messrs Fore Bros.,
Memphis, Texas

Gentlemen:

Please fill out the following order & get it out to our Headquarter Ranche on North Elm Creek as soon as possible. We believe our order will just about make a load for a two horse wagon: the freight rate of 60c is abominally high, for we can get freight hauled from Childress at any time for 50c & from there they have to cross Red River: do your utmost to get this rate of 60c lowered.

Take care that you put none of the articles ordered in paper sacks & mind that the flour is good for we shall sample it, & if bad return it. . . Mind that the fruit you send is good & not wormy, we shall examine it, & if bad return it. Also see that the molasses is in reality New Orleans molasses, we will not receive anything else.

1 sack green coffee
250 lbs canvassed strip bacon. (not Armour's)
150 lbs granulated sugar
1000 lbs Wichita best high patent Flour
2 ten gallon kegs New Orleans Mollasses
2 cases Lard, 5 lb tins if possible; if not, 10
150 lbs Navy Beans
100 lbs California Prunes
50 lbs Dried Peaches
6 boxes Axel Greese
25 lbs Rice
150 lbs Corn Meal
10 lb can best Mustard (Coleman's if possible)
10 gallons vinegar (not acid)
6 cases canned Corn
6 cases canned Tomatoes
3 cases canned Okra & Tomatoes mixed
1 case Coal oil

Truly yours,

Rocking Chair Ranche Limd
By A J M

Provisions order by Rocking Chair Ranch manager A.J. Marjoribanks

FOUR WAYS TEXANS MADE COFFEE WITHOUT COFFEE

1.

We would parch okra seed, barley meal, or anything we could get and make coffee.

Mrs. M.E.F. Mackey, explaining settlers' poverty in post-Civil War Texas, *Dallas Semi Weekly Farm News*, date unknown

2.

Mrs. [Mary] New cut up sweet potatoes in small bits, strung them on a string, dried them and parched them like coffee. Then they were ground in the old coffee mill. There you are—sweet potato coffee. In some sections the pioneers used barley for coffee.

T.U. Taylor, Austin, 1941

3.

For coffee they used a mixture of cracked and parched post oak acorns, rye and wheat grains.

T.U. Taylor, Austin, 1941

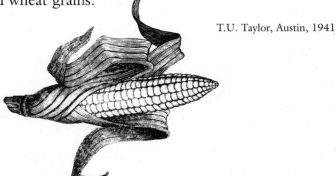

4.

Such a thing as a real cup of coffee was not to be had at all. Instead they roasted corn and acorns and mixed certain portions together and used it.

A. Huffmeyer, "Adventures of an Old Texas Cowboy," 1941

TEXAS EATS

Orange Blossom Muffins

1 slightly beaten egg

1/4 cup sugar

1/2 cup orange juice

2 tablespoons salad oil or melted shortening

2 cups biscuit mix

1/2 cup orange marmalade

1/2 cup chopped pecans

Combine first four ingredients; add biscuit mix and beat vigorously for 30 seconds. Stir in marmalade and pecans. Grease muffin pans or line with paper baking cups; fill 2/3 full.

Topping:
1/4 cup sugar

1 1/2 tablespoons flour

1/2 teaspoon cinnamon

1/4 teaspoon nutmeg

1 tablespoon butter

Combine sugar, flour, nutmeg, and cinnamon; cut in butter until mixture is crumbly. Sprinkle over batter in each muffin cup. Bake at 400 degrees for 20 to 25 minutes. Makes 1 dozen.

Legendary breakfast muffin recipe from Jefferson's historic Excelsior House hotel restaurant

THREE TALES OF THE PECOS HIGH BRIDGE

1. A Woman Was First to Ride the Rails

The high, spindle-legged railroad bridge across the deep canyon formed by the Pecos River between Langtry and Comstock was breathtaking. It was more breathtaking to stand on it and look down than to stand beneath it and look up. It had no guardrails, and a broad footpath ran its length. To walk across made one giddy enough, and legend gives credit to a young ranchwoman who first dared to ride across it on horseback. She was celebrated in an anonymous poem, "The Pecos River Queen."

James Cooper of Snyder said that when he lived near the bridge in the 1930s, sheet metal was laid in places where the wooden walk was unsafe. Many times, however, he and others rode their horses across that clattering path with the danger of plummeting to death at both elbows. He said you needed a steady, unspookable horse.

Others told stories of their encounters with the Old Pecos High Bridge. When she was a child, Katherine Anne Porter crossed it more than once on trips from Kyle, Texas, to El Paso. She remembered the bridge, which was two years younger than she, having been built in 1892, as being unsafe. She wrote, "Here was the famous and beautiful Pecos Bridge, then supposed to be the highest and one of the longest in the world." Three hundred twenty-one feet above the river, it stretched 2,180 feet long, almost half a mile. It was the highest bridge in the United States and third highest in the world, merely 27 feet short of the record.

Elton Miles, *More Tales from the Big Bend*, 1988

2. The train stopped at the edge of

the bridge and we looked down into this great chasm and wondered at the long slender spidery legs that held up this bridge that we were going to cross. Everybody got out except the engineer and fireman. All of us, carrying our light luggage and suitcases, walked across the bridge. All of us arrived on the other side and waited as the train came after us and we stood watching, I remember, this train crossing this shambling bridge; you could see it shaking and the train wobbling from side to side. Nothing happened. The train arrived and after the last wheel was on firm ground, we all climbed back and proceeded with our journey. Grandmother and I did this three times. I wonder what became of that bridge.

Katherine Anne Porter, *Atlantic Monthly,* March 1975;
A new bridge was built in the mid-1940s and
the old bridge torn down soon after.

★ ★ ★ ★ ★ ★ ★ ★ ★ ★ ★ ★ ★ ★ ★ ★

The [Pecos] river would give a killdee that flew over it diarrhea.

Assessment of the Pecos' sour water by an
early rancher, quoted by Dee Brown in
Wondrous Times on the Frontier, 1991

★ ★ ★ ★ ★ ★ ★ ★ ★ ★ ★ ★ ★ ★ ★ ★

3. *The Pecos River Queen*

Where the Pecos River winds and twists
on its journey to the sea
from its white walls of sand and rock
striving ever to be free.

Near the highest railroad bridge
that all these modern days are seen
swells fair young Patti Moorehead
The Pecos River Queen.

She was known by every cowboy
on the Pecos River wide
that knew full well that she could shoot
that she could rope and ride.

She could rope and tie
as quick as any man
she was voted by all cowboys
as number one top cowhand.

Across the Comstock railroad bridge
the highest in the west
Patti rode her horse one day
her lover's heart to test.

For he told her he would
brave all dangers for her sake,
but the puncher would not follow
so she is still without a mate.

Anonymous, printed in *From Darkness into Light*,
by Mildred Adams, 1978

ESCAPE FROM INDIANS WAS IN THE STARS

The Civil War began when Martha Gray was very small but she recalls a few circumstances during that time. Men were either in the ranger service or in the war while women at home shouldered the heavy burdens. She says: "When quite young I was taught to fear the Comanche Indians and to watch any strange object moving, for Indians sometimes crawled or walked in most any way to fool the people. We learned to fear any strange noise. We were taught to identify the north star and the Big Dipper in case we got lost from home or might be carried away by Indians. By knowing these heavenly bodies we could find the easterly direction and travel in that direction. The Indians lived to the west."

Martha Gray, Lometa, Texas,
interviewed for the *Frontier Times*,
September 1941

TEXAS LOST ★ ★ ★ ★ ★ ★ ★ ★
Bebe, Texas

Not entirely lost, but severely diminished in size and importance, Bebe remains a little town on Texas 97 in southwest Gonzales County. What Bebe actually has lost is a couple of "E's." When founded in 1909, the place was stuck for a name. At that time, the BeeBee Baking Soda Company had advertised itself liberally around the county. The name had a certain euphonious sound, so citizens adopted it, and sometime later, discarded a pair of superfluous "E's."

11

A FESTIVE TEXAS TO-DO

A thoroughly enjoyable series of revels was celebrated last Thursday at the ranch of Capt. Keith Gordon near Junction City in Kimble county, a general invitation having been extended to the whole countryside, and handsome prizes offered by the captain and various friends for the different race contests. . . On the eve of the feast the barbers were busy furbishing up the young ranchmen, who then bought all the available hats and gloves and cooled their ardor by refrigerated fluids. All along the Llano river at night camp fires were passed, and at the ranch a couple of beeves and four sheep were roasting over a charcoal fire. Early next morning, wagons, buggies, ambulances and equestrians began to assemble, and soon animated groups were formed beneath the shade of the fine pecans and oaks, the lemonade stand, provided with half a ton of ice, drove a thriving trade, and the marvels of the phonograph delighted numbers who for the first time listened to strains of bottled harmony.

Descending a steep and shaded slope we came on the broad stream of the North Llano, both banks begirt by broad woods of stately sycamores, live oaks and towering pecan trees, the beauty of the vista in either direction being unsurpassed and seldom equaled. In this enchanted sylvan retreat, was an enormous dining table 100 feet long, whilst adjacent boards supplies were prepared, the indefatigable Messrs. Prentis and Braggins carving beef and mutton for fully 600 hungry mouths, whilst the latter's wife directed the lady assistants.

Two broad and level race tracts, one of 1200 yards and the other of a quarter of a mile, were marked by over a hundred gay streamers, flags of all nations and nondescript banners of fluttering bunting. The 150 yard foot race for the championship of the county was well contested and a hat and belt awarded to Mr. Pierce Keaton, a stalwart young ranchman of the neighborhood. The tournament or tilting contest was exceedingly interesting, the prize falling to Mr. Conway Younger, who bore off six out of a possible nine rings on his lance's point. . .

But the most amusing contest for the spectators was the needle and thread race, a dozen cavaliers riding headlong amid clouds of blinding dust at a rope barrier, where dismounting, they rushed afoot to their ladies some 100 yards distant who had then to thread each her needle which the respective Knights had then, having reversed their steeds, to bear back to the starting point. Some ladies were so pestered by ardent admirers that they were too nervous to thread their needles, one had been given a needle without an eye, several horses bolted while others became so restive their owners could not mount. However, shrieks of laughter were produced by these mishaps and all were thoroughly amused.

The Southern Messenger, August 17, 1893

TEXANESE

Ol' Slick Legs

Referred, usually, to a pretty young girl, "Ol'" was a term of affection, not an indicator of age. The young woman, invariably single and pursued by suitors, also was called "heifer" and "sweet thing" and "filly" and "little lady."

MR. WASSON TELLS ABOUT HIS LIFE

Hello this is Melvin S. Wasson this is my life as I remember it. I was born in lawerance county Arkansas which is in the Northeast part of Arkansas. I am the youngest of 6 children 4 girls and two boys. I came to Texas in a covered wagon with my parents and my brothers and 4 sisters there was 2 other familys with us and there were wagons. I was 9 years old and this was in May of 1898 it took about a month to make the trip. We came through the Indian Terrytory which is now Oklahoma. I remember we had Indians follow us during the day and they would stay just so far away. They never did bother us but the men dident take any chances the men would take turns in standing guard at night. We would put the wagons in a kind of circle at night. . . When we came to the Arkansas river we crossed it on a Pontoon Bridge. That Brings Us to Our new home 3 1/2 miles North West of Plainview, Texas. Dad came out there in 1897 and bought a Section of land it had a nice orchard and vinyard a windmill cow shed correll and a 3 barbed wire fence all around and a 1/2 Dougout and he made his living off the orchard and vinyard he (didn't) do any farming. Well when we got there we had to live in our wagons and the 1/2 dougout till Dad got a house built. So he got busy and got a building contract and began building a house it had 6 rooms. My Dad had to have some cattle so he bought a hurd from a man named Dick Hudgins. I don't know how many cattle he bought but he got quite a few he gave $3.50 for each cow and the calf was throghed in for good measure. And the next year or So dad bought the section joining the home Section on the west for $800. Oh yes I was about to forget to say how much Dad paid for the home Section he paid $750.00 just A Little over $1.00 per acre.

Melvin S. Wasson, quoted in *Hale County: Facts and Folklore*, by Vera Dean Wofford, 1978

★ ★ ★ ★ ★ ★ ★ ★ ★ ★ ★ ★ ★ ★ ★ ★ ★ ★

HORSES HAVE THE RIGHT-OF-WAY

Section 3. Any person driving or operating an automobile or motor vehicle shall at the request, or signal by putting up the hand, or by other visible signals from a person riding or driving a horse or horses or other domestic animal or animals, cause such vehicle or machine to come to a standstill as quickly as possible and remain stationary long enough to allow such animal or animals to pass.

Dalhart city ordinance, passed December 12, 1919

ONE BROTHER WRITES TO ANOTHER IN 1860

Burnet
Burnet Co., Texas

Frank:

I received your letter today dated 10th of March, which I now endeavor to answer. I was glad to hear that you were well received.

We have had a good deal of Indian excitement since you left. I think there have been at least five Indians killed here since you left. Proctor's negro (Bob) and the Widow Allen's negro man (Joe) were up at town to see their wives, and started home one Monday morning just before day, and when they got down opposite Mr. Baker's they were attacked by about 12 Indians. The Indians charged on them, but Bob was riding a tolerably good horse and the Indians could not catch him, but they got close enough to shoot him in the head [but] did not penetrate it. Old Joe's pony was rather slow and the Indians soon ran up to him, but went up so close that when the Indians would go to shoot, old Joe would grab the arrows and throw them down to the ground; and the Indian that was contending with Joe got tired of this game and aimed to strike Joe on the head with his bow. But Joe caught the arrow as he struck at him, and drew the Indian to him and knocked him off his horse with his fist, and made his escape. The whites followed the Indians and succeeded in killing two and wounding some others.

There have been other events in regard to Indians which I will mention in my next. Billy and I have been out every time the Indians have come in, but have never got into a fight. I will leave the Indian subject.

Norfleet has moved into the post [Fort Croghan]. I suppose they were afraid. The children are all going to school. . .

I have been taking care of your mare and colts since the Indians were in.

There are but few people here and everything is dull.
Goodbye

Letter from J.M. Thomas to his brother, Frank, April 5, 1860

The first mule ever born in Lampasas county. . . is 44 years old. Steve Smith says he has known the mule since 1895, and she was four years old at the time. The mule, named Mag, is now blind and hard of hearing, but she eats three times a day. Bran, oats and cottonseed meal are her rations and she can gobble up ten ears of corn as fast as any animal alive. She is branded U on the shoulder.

Mag has had a varied career. Once a rider won $300 betting that she could out-race a pony at Goldthwaite. The pony was almost suffocated by mule dust. Again she has taken part in rodeos as a roping animal. Five years ago part of her tail dropped off. Old age was setting in. She stands in the shade of the trees, a cheap but effective drunk. Her original weight was 850 pounds, but it has dropped now to 650. For fifteen years she has done nothing but give out interviews to visitors who believe she is the oldest mule alive in the United States. Once a boy shot out an eye with a target rifle, and then the light in the other disappeared. For four years, she has been totally blind. She has never had but one owner and that is Cornelius McAnelley, the founder of McAnelley's Bend. Mr. McAnelley is confined to his wheel chair now but he is brought out in the yard at times to caress his ancient companion.

Sam Ashburn, writing in the *San Angelo Morning Times*, June 1934

KILLER TEXAS CHICKENS

I have personally seen chickens kill and eat rattlesnakes. In the summer of 1928 I was living at 1120 Burr Road on the northern outskirts of San Antonio, Texas. One evening I caught a female rattlesnake as it was sleeping on a brush pile. I caught the snake by the tail as I had no other means of getting it, and carried it back to the house and put it in a box. I judged from her appearance that she had recently given birth to some young snakes and in a few days four were killed. Each had one button only. Two were killed and eaten by some of my chickens, which weighed not more than three pounds. Going out in the chicken yard that morning I saw a Cochin China pullet with a young rattlesnake in her beak pursued by the rest of the chickens and muscovey ducks. In order that other witnesses might see this unusual performance I called to a neighbor and his wife and his cook and to my wife and cook, so that we would have six witnesses. By the time they arrived the pullet had evidently swallowed the young rattlesnake, but a Plymouth Rock cockerel had another, and he was being pursued like the pullet. My witnesses having arrived, I ran the chicken down until he dropped the snake. It was a young Texas diamondback rattler (*Crotalus atrox*) about twelve inches long, and it was still alive. I cut it in three pieces with an ax and the chickens and muscovey ducks fought over it greedily until every piece was swallowed.

Col. M.L. Crimmins, *Bulletin of the Antivenom Institute of America*, September 1931

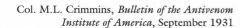

A REDUNDANCY OF PERCEIVED TEXAS HUMOR

• Texas nursery rhyme: the butcher, the baker, the Cadillac maker. . .

• A Texan at a Nassau beach ran over to a crowd and found that his wife was being revived. He asked what they were doing to her and the guard said, *"We're going to give her artificial respiration."* The Texan replied, *"Artificial, hell! Give her the real thing. I can afford it."*

• Watching a recently departing oil rich Texan buried in his air-conditioned Cadillac, according to his last request, a near-rich relative commented, *"Yep, that's what I call livin'."*

• Texas housewife to husband: *"Will you get out the car, dear, and drive the children to the backyard so they can play."*

• Did you hear about the rich Texas woman who has two chinchilla wraps—one for each chin?

• Cute little blonde talking to wealthy Texan: *"How much did you say your name was?"*

• When a Texas class was told that the next day they would learn to draw, eighteen youngsters showed up with pistols.

• *"You don't mean to tell me that you have 365 days of sunshine in Texas every year?"* asked a visitor, and the native son replied, *"I shore do, and that is a mighty conservative estimate."*

• Boasted the Texas cattleman to the visitor: *"We don't brand them. We have them engraved."*

• The middle-aged Texan went to the psychiatrist and begged, *"Doc, I shore need your help. I'm in a bad way. I been a Texan all my life and suddenly I just don't give a damn!"*

Stewart Harral, *When It's Laughter You're After*, 1962

HOW TO CURE RUSTLING

Rustling became a well organized business [mid-1880s] in many sections of the range country. Coryell co., and its vicinity, was one of the localities where a tolerable lot of rustler trouble existed.

The condition became so bad that the ranchers were forced to organize and deal with the situation directly. Committees were organized to handle the rustlers. Those committees would notify a rustler to leave the community or desist his business. If the party failed to heed the demand, then the committee would catch the accused and hold a trial.

The trials were under a kangaroo court arrangement. One member of the committee would act as the judge, another the prosecutor. The evidence for and against would be heard. The verdict would be rendered according to the majority of the committee. Many were sentenced to be hanged and the hanging would take place on the spot. Some of the accused were turned loose with a warning and given another chance.

The actions of the committees in Coryell co., had a wholesome effect on the rustlers and their depredations were checked considerably.

The Library of Congress, WPA Writers Project; from interview with cowboy/rancher A.M. Garrett of Fort Worth, age 83, February 23, 1934

WILDFLOWERS AND PINTO BEANS

The prettiest wildflowers I've seen this spring along a highway are between Fredericksburg and Mason. It's a great year for prickly pear white poppies. On that Fredericksburg-Mason highway the poppies sometimes make the pastures look like fields of open cotton.

The best Bluebonnets I've seen are growing in a place I never expected them, and in one sense that's too bad because very few folks will get to enjoy them. They're blooming in an outrageous way along several miles of a dirt road west and south of Mason. It's the county road we use to reach our James River campsite here on the Schulze Ranch. . .

I grew up on land like this, but I never before saw rocky, brushy hillsides covered with Bluebonnets. Blossoms so thick they seem artificial. . . The color in places is so intense the land seems to heave in blue and white and pink waves. I wish you could see it.

We've been coming here. . .on the James River several years. Right now we are four. The others are off fishing, and I won't see them until the pinto beans are done. . .

I volunteered to stay in camp and cook beans this morning. I pretended it was a sacrifice, but the truth is I needed the solitude to get this report done. Also I like being here. . .cooking beans and listening to the music of the river and the birds and the wind. I feel good here.

I have invested a lot of myself into these beans. I want them to be good. I want them to be bragged on. I want somebody to say "Best beans ever cooked on a river bank and stirred with a screwdriver." I may say that myself if nobody else does. . .

I am fixing way too many beans. Four pounds, dry weight. But I brought my great restaurant-kitchen pot, and you can't, with any good grace, cook two cups of beans in a pot that big. Two cups would insult it. The beans are coming along, but they lack something. Wish I had an onion about the size of a Pecos cantaloupe.

Did I mention the yucca blooms? They are on the face of the cliff across the river from camp. . . From a distance they give the image of big creamy white faces, staring out of the brush. We are talking about a plant sometimes 14 inches tall, making a cluster of flowers 2 feet long and 10 inches wide. From this rock I count ninety-three of them across the river.

The beans are getting better, but they still lack character. I am thinking about pouring two cups of red wine in them. What do you think?

Leon Hale, *Texas Chronicles*, 1989

TEXAS EATS

Red Bean Pie

1 cup cooked, mashed pinto beans

1 cup sugar

3 egg yolks, beaten

1 cup milk

1 teaspoon vanilla

1 teaspoon nutmeg

Combine ingredients and place in uncooked pie crust. Bake at 350 degrees for 30 minutes or until set. Make meringue with leftover egg whites; spread on pie and brown in oven.

Cowpoke's Cookbook, by Ace Reid, Draggin' S Ranch, Kerrville, Texas, 1969

Turkey Fries
(Just As Good As Calf Fries)

Editor's Note: for the uninitiated, turkey fries, like calf fries, are testicles, only smaller.

Clean and rinse the Turkey Fries (as many as required).
Dry on paper towels.
Make a batter of:
2 cups biscuit mix

3/4 cup milk

3/4 cup club soda

2 eggs, slightly beaten

Mix until batter is fairly smooth. If batter does not adhere to meat good, add more biscuit mix. Fry in hot oil until golden brown.

More Calf Fries to Caviar, 1988

A DEATH OVER SAUERKRAUT

It was high noon in the town of Ogalalla, Nebraska, the 6th day of August, 1877. A.I. (Babe) Moye. . .and a dozen more Texas cowboys were seated at a table in a restaurant enjoying the noon meal. It was while the party were engaged with their meal that there sauntered into the room a man by the name of Bill Campbell. Campbell hung his hat on a nail, spoke to some of the boys he knew, and later made an uncomplimentary remark about a dish the party was eating—sauerkraut. Hardly had he finished his remark than it was excepted to by Babe Moye, and in a manner that could leave no doubt in mind of anyone but what he meant what he said. Moye's remarks brought forth a sharp retort from Campbell, with the final result that it was agreed they would meet over at the saloon across the street and shoot it out after they finished the meal.

By a strange coincidence neither Campbell or Moye was armed at the time, otherwise the quarrel would have been settled then and there. Moye soon walked out of the restaurant, going across the street to the hotel, where his brother, Andy, Monroe Hinton, Capt. Gosman, and W.G. Butler, were seated at a table figuring up some final details of a cattle sale.

Babe Moye came in very abruptly and called for a pistol, and from his actions, his friends knew trouble was brewing. No one offered to let Moye have a pistol and he whirled around and walked out, followed by Andy [and the other men]. Babe Moye walked straight across the street and entered the rear door of the saloon. He walked boldly up to Campbell and without a word slapped Campbell in the breast with his left hand.

Campbell immediately drew his pistol and [fired] at Moye. Andy Moye, a witness to what was going on, and thinking Campbell had shot his brother, suddenly jerked his pistol and fired before Campbell could shoot again. His aim was perfect and the ball entered Campbell's breast—a death shot. Both men then advanced on each other, shooting as they approached. Finally Andy Moye and Campbell clinched and continued shooting until both pistols were empty, and the latter crumbled on the floor stone dead, and with five bullet wounds through his body.

When the smoke of the battle cleared away, Monroe Hinton was found to have two bullet wounds—one through his body and one through his leg. Campbell was dead and W.G. Butler had been struck in the thigh by a stray bullet. Capt. Gosman's life was saved by a watch he carried in his vest pocket. . .

Andy was never indicted for the killing of Campbell, as it was considered that he had shot Campbell believing that Campbell had shot his brother and was acting in the defense of his brother's life.

Kenedy, Texas, *Advance*,
September 2, 1926

✪ ✪ ✪ ✪ ✪ ✪ ✪ ✪ ✪ ✪ ✪ ✪ ✪ ✪ ✪ ✪ ✪ ✪ ✪

TEXAS WEATHER'S A LITTLE IMMODERATE

Increased ranching brought more and more people to northwest Texas, a vast, flat prairie of titanic weather forms. Blasting by tornadoes was one frequent hazard; another was dust storms. . . .Winters could be bitter, the most regular event was the "norther," and nowhere in Texas were they more abrupt than on the treeless plains: [one rancher wrote] "First, a chilly whiff; then a puff, the grass bends flat, and, bang, it is upon us, a blast that would have taken a top-gallant sail smack out of the boltropes, and cold as if blowing across a sea of ice. We galloped to the nearest ravine, and hurried on all the clothing we could muster. A thermometer. . .showed a fall of sixty degrees in seven hours."

James Haley,
Texas: An Album of History, 1985

TEXANESE
Air-Tights

Range food mostly was fresh, meaning cowboys ate what they could kill with, perhaps, the addition of dried beans, biscuits or cornbread. When commercial canning was begun in the 1870s, cowboy fare became slightly more varied and foodstuffs like tomatoes and peaches could be brought along. Because the canning process involved preserving food in a vacuum, the cans were called air-tights. In some instances the term was applied to a man who was blustery and windy because the cans often made a whooshing sound when opened.

A STYLISH SEAT

A good saddle would cost the cowboy from forty to one hundred dollars. In his boyish notions of economy, to want a thing was to have it if he had the money, and a saddle once seen and coveted had most to do with its cost. The Spanish saddles of the Southwest were often heavily decorated with silver, as were the bits, spurs, and bridle reins, as well as the clothing of the rider; but this sort of foppery never prevailed to any extent among American cowpunchers. There was one rude and wild sort of decoration sometimes in practice by the younger cowboys on the range. They often took the skins of rattlesnakes, of which there were very many seen nearly every day, and spread them while yet wet upon the leather of their saddles. The natural glue of the skin would hold it firmly in place when it dried. Some saddles have been fairly covered with these lines of diamond-marked skins. It was not uncommon to see the skins of these snakes also used as hat bands.

E. Hough, *The Story of the Cowboy*, 1897

TEXANESE
Pimple

A scoffing term for one of those little bitty sissy saddles used by eastern riders, the kind with no horn, small seat pad and short stirrups. Also called a "pancake" or "pumpkin seed."

What I remember about the *dust storms of the 30s. . .* is a choking, suffocating sensation, a feeling of being swallowed up by the elements. On the open prairie there is not the sound of wind in trees or very little about the eaves of houses or buildings. Then, too, the dusters rolled in on a calm of a wind change, or perhaps the bigger eye of a hurricane. . . Sleeping and waking what I recall is a soughing sound, as an indrawn breath, more like the ebbing of a wave on the shore rather than the breaking of its crest. Sometimes the dust-cloud came in like an ocean wave, with the dirt falling out of its crest before the wind of the full wave hit. But most of the first ones came in as rolling clouds. It has seemed to me since that they were like tornadoes carried horizontally by a prevailing wind. And, strangely, we had very few tornadoes in this area in the dust storm years.

When the dusters came from the west or southwest, they were more reddish or sand colored. Those had a more grinding sound, as of teeth being set on edge. . .We took cover whenever possible. We had to light our lamps. But I do not recall any work accomplished while the wind blew except cooking, and that in covered pots.

Nova Blair, from her letter, July 11, 1985, quoted in *Blessed Assurance*, 1987

★ ★

WINDY TALE

I arrived in Dalhart just before sundown. Pebbles as big as the end of my thumb—that's no lie—struck me in the face, and the wind blew for three days and nights. I had to shovel my way to bed at night.

George Barrett, remembering the blowing
sand and wind of the Texas Panhandle in 1901,
quoted by Lillie Mae Hunter, *The Book of Years*, 1967

A FEW MEMORIES OF TEXAS' SECOND OLDEST LIVING SLAVE

Nellie Wardlaw Smith was born in 1825 near Pine Bluff, Arkansas, on the Lewis Wardlaw plantation. Wardlaw moved to Falls County, Texas, in 1857, bringing his family and 15 slaves, including Nellie Smith.

"We settled about five miles from the Brazos near Reagan, and lived in camp style until we could build our houses. Some of the men cut down trees and cleared land while the women followed along and burned the brush. The best trees were used to make logs for the houses. As soon as the land was cleared we planted corn and cotton.

"We did not know what a cook stove was in them days: I never saw one until I was a middle aged woman. We cooked on large fireplaces; some of them was large enough to use eight foot sticks of wood. There were iron cranes at each end of the fireplace. We hung the pots on them and swung them back over the fire. You could not go off and leave your dinner for fear a pot might turn over and spill your grub. We baked pretty, yellow poundcakes in the ovens that sat on legs over the fire. Taters baked in the ashes was hard to beat. . .

"My ole Massa was a hard worker; he worked along in the field beside us. We went to the field early in the morning. There was a black man to blow the horn to get the slaves up way 'fore day.

"We worked from 'fore daylight till dark. I had my 400 pounds of cotton to pick every day.

"Ole Massa whipped me once 'cause I did not drop the corn right. We had to learn to check corn so that it was easier to plow. I could not learn it right at first and he beat me good. Soon after that he sent me to the 'big house' to help nurse the children and do some of the house work.

"My old Missus would weave and sew for the slaves. She carded the cotton into rolls and spun it into yarn and reel the yarn into hanks. . . Ole Missus could weave about twelve yards of cloth in a day. We got two sets of clothing a year—one in the spring and one in the fall. We had heavy underwear, and did not get cold. Nearly all of our clothes were white. We had 'Russett Brogans' and 'coarse' shoes. Missus knitted stockings and socks for us.

"My Massa was a Baptist, and we all went to meeting under the brush arbor once a month. The white people sat near the front and the black people in the back. Mr. Putty preached to us. We could not read nor write but we loved to hear him read the Bible. . .

"Ole Massa would let us dance and have a good time when the work was laid by. We had a man who could play the fiddle and we had a good time. Sometimes he would give us a 'black and white' [a furlough pass] and let us go to the adjoining plantation. If we did not have this paper the patrol would whip us and take us back home.

"Ole Massa was getting ready to go enlist in the Confederate Army along in '63 when he died. We did not have any trouble during the war. One day [son] John Wardlaw called us all up to the house and told us we was just like him; we were free, and we could stay with him, and he would pay us. We was lost like a chicken from his mammy. We stayed on with the Wardlaw family for a while and then we moved on Mr. Churchill Jones' plantation."

Interview with "Aunt Nellie" Smith of Marlin, age 107, in *Frontier Times*, December 1932

CATTLE HIDES BUILT TEXAS

It used to be a saying that what a Texan can't mend with rawhide "ain't worth mending." Before "bobwire" became popular as twine, Texans according to another saying was "held together with rawhide." It was well bound. Some people called the binding "Mexican Iron." It was an essential factor in the culture of the country. . .

Seasoned Texans came to be known in some parts as "rawhides." The Texas cowhand, if he did not expect to return at night to the place where he saddled his horse in the morning, carried his rawhide hobbles either on his saddle or, more frequently, around his horse's neck—like a bell strap, which was also of rawhide.

In 1868 Jim Loving struck out from Parker County, Texas, with 2,600 head of cattle and 20 cowboys, for Colorado. One day while he was in the Indian territory, a Comanche chief with about a thousand warriors halted the herd. Immediately he accused Loving and his men of being Texans—in Comanche, as in Mexican, minds a nationality apart and distinct from Americans. Loving did his best to convince the Comanche that his outfit was from Kansas. He was making out a pretty good case when a warrior noticed the pair of rawhide hobbles around the neck of a horse ridden by one of Loving's men.

"Tejano!" he growled, pointing to the hobbles and then twitching the Texan's nose.

The Indians took a lot of cattle though the Texas men escaped with the main herd and their lives. Rawhide gave them away. . .

A class of Texans, not highly respected, were called "rawhiders." Before setting out on any trip, the migratory rawhiders "usually killed three or four large steers, not for food, but for hides." These were stored in their wagon beds and supplied a hundred and one needs. If they had a breakdown, they soaked the hide and cut it into long strips, called whangs, which they wrapped around the broken hub, wheel, or tongue. As the whang dried, the edges of the break drew together. Their chairs, camp stools, wheelbarrows and buckets were made from hide. Their oxen were shod with it, and the shoes they themselves wore were usually made from leftover pieces. . .

It was the domestic use of rawhide by pioneers that made it a component of American culture. One of the earliest school teachers among the Texas colonists on the Brazos river was W.W. Browning. He used to tell of a certain experience he had in trying to teach one of the young Texans how to spell "bed." Finally in desperation he asked the blockhead, "What do you sleep on at night?"

"Cowhides and blankets," came the prompt reply. . .

[Rancher] Charlie Goodnight used to tell about a traveler on the frontier who stopped at an old-timer's ranch for the night. After supper and a smoke, the host yanked a "beef hide" from the corner of the cabin, threw it upon the dirt floor, turned to the traveler and said, "You sleep here, I'll rough it."

"As tough as rawhide," the old saying went. Probably no form of animal structure excepting teeth and ivory was ever tougher than the dried hide of an old Longhorn bull. The ultimate in "guying," "ragging," deviling a human being was appropriately termed "rawhiding." To rawhide or cowhide man or beast in a more literal sense was to "beat the living daylights out of him."

J. Frank Dobie, *Houston Post*, 1941

BOWIE'S MYTHOLOGICAL KNIFE

The Bowie knife was the New World's counterpart to the battle-axe with which Beowulf slew Grendel in the den deep under dark waters; to Siegfried's great sword Gram; and to King Arthur's bright Excalibur of mystic powers.

Who devised the Bowie knife? Who made it. . . ?

The two witnesses nearest to [Jim] Bowie contradict each other on the knife's origin but agree on the event that gave it fame. In 1838, only two years after the fall of the Alamo, [brother] Rezin P. Bowie wrote, from Iberville, Louisiana, a flaming letter to the editor of *The Planters' Advocate* to refute a "dastardly scribbler's" story about the Bowie brothers and the knife. "The first Bowie Knife," he said, "was made by myself in the parish of Avoyelles, in this state, as a hunting knife, for which purpose, exclusively, it was used for many years" before James drove it "as a weapon of defense into an individual with whom he was at variance." The phrase, "made by myself," was an abbreviated way of saying that Rezin P. Bowie had his blacksmith make the knife.

In 1858, *De Bow's Review* published a remarkably frank sketch by [still another brother] John J. Bowie on the Bowies of Louisiana. According to John J., his brother James, while living mostly in the woods, had a blacksmith named Lovel Snowden make him the "hunting knife". . . He had a "neat scabbard" made for the knife, "affirming that he would wear it as long as he lived, which he did."

The weight of testimony is on the side of Rezin P. Bowie's account. . .

The size of the original knife will always be in question. Rezin P. Bowie wrote that "the length [of the blade] was nine and one quarter inches, its width one and a half inches, single edge, and not curved." Other specifiers go on up to eighteen, even twenty-four inches. The knife probably had a buckhorn handle. Proportion, balance and temper of steel went into its superiority. A curved point became a feature of the Bowie knife.

J. Frank Dobie, *Tales of Old Time Texas*, 1928
(There are several other less credible stories about the knife's origin; truth is, nobody knows for sure.)

TEXAS EATS

Christmas Cornbread Dressing

5 or 6 cups chicken or turkey broth

1 pan of corn bread

7 or 8 biscuits

1 or 3 eggs, hard-boiled

1 medium size onion, chopped

2/3 cup chopped celery

1/2 tsp. salt

1/2 tsp. sage

1/4 tsp. black pepper

Cook onion and celery in broth for about five minutes. Crumble corn bread and biscuit with pepper and sage. Add to mixture, stirring until all bread is moist and soft. Add chopped boiled eggs. Beat by hand for one or two minutes. Dressing should be rather soft. Pour in a 2 quart baking dish and cook in oven at 400 degrees for 45 to 50 minutes, or stuff inside the holiday bird.

Louise Dillow & Deenie Carver,
Mrs. Blackwell's Heart of Texas Cookbook, 1980

HIYO SILVER WAS A TEXAN!

In the very first screen production, "The Lone Ranger" (A Republic serial), there were five actors that wore the familiar. . . mask and rode a beautiful white horse. . .

It is interesting to note that when [creator George] Trendle gave his okay for Republic to produce the serial that there were certain qualifications that the studio had to follow before allowing their choice to be seen by the movie audience. Trendle specified that the actor be a clean-shaven, rugged outdoors type of a man, height not to be less than five foot eleven and weight of approximately 170 pounds; the white Stetson, bootshod, but chapless Lone Ranger was not to swear or drink and could only smoke if the plot demanded. . . On Tonto's requirements it was a bit different with the same general terms except that the Indian should be several inches shorter than the Lone Ranger. Trendle even went as far as describing the requirements for the equally famous mounts of these two heroes. (Silver as approximating the characteristics of an Arabian stallion not less than 15 1/2 hands high; Republic found that the hardest role to fill was that of "Silver.")

A casting interview for horses was held. Thirty-five of the most beautiful white stallions in Hollywood were brought into the studio. They were all put through their paces and judged on ability to obey commands and beauty. None of them would do.

Robert Beche, in charge of this unusual job, heard of a white stallion that would be perfect for the role, but the horse was in El Paso, Texas. Beche was shown photographs of the animal and was so impressed that he immediately made arrangements with American Airlines for the horse to be flown to Hollywood in a special transport plane.

Silver arrived safely and was exactly the type of animal Beche demanded.

Mario DeMarco, The Lone Rangers of the Silver Screen and Television, undated but about 1983

★ ★ ★ ★ ★ ★ ★ ★ ★ ★ ★ ★ ★ ★ ★ ★ ★

"TEXAS"

Name of Teddy Roosevelt's horse ridden as he led his Rough Riders across Cuba during the Spanish-American War of 1898. "Texas" came from Seguin, outside San Antonio, and was acquired by Roosevelt while he was in the Alamo City recruiting for his soldier corps in the bar of the Menger Hotel.

Oh, I am a Texas cowboy, right off the Texas plains.
My trade is cinchin' saddles and pullin' of bridle reins,
And I can throw a lasso with the greatest of ease;
I can rope and ride a bronco any damn way I please.

MESSAGE UNDERWEAR ON THE FRONTIER

The older woman remembers well the flour-sack days of Texas, and she doesn't have to be so old, either. The sheets, the pillowcases, the tablecloths, the dishtowels, the children's underwear, the doilies and the antimacassars and center-table covers, the jelly-strainers, milk-strainers, pudding bags, and overnight cases! Miles of Mexican drawn work went into the flour-sack cloth, miles of hemstitching and tiny tucks, millions of fine, painstaking stitches. The flour sack played a major role in the Texas woman's household economy and art of living.

"I married John," a little lady, now a sprightly seventy-five, often tells, "and I came to Texas to take what might befall. I had been brought up in Philadelphia and been trained for a musical career, so I'd hardly washed a dish or mended a stocking before I came to Texas. But it was all such fun! After two years in our camp my trousseau clothes began to wear out. My dresses were of good, strong material, and I had mended them here and there where the brush had torn them, so that they did very nicely. But my underwear had got quite beyond mending.

"So one day I asked John about it. 'John,' I said, 'do you think you could get me a few yards of white material at the store the next time you go to town?"

'Honey,' he said, 'I wish I could, but we've barely enough for some things I need for the sheep, and I don't want to ask Schreiner [Kerrville general store] for another dollar till I've paid something back. Could you possibly wait till the wool is sold this fall?'

"I give you my word that I hadn't heard of flour-sack underwear at the time. I had seen very little of women in those two years. So I thought my idea was quite original. I took two flour sacks and fashioned a pair of drawers. Such work as went into them! I always did like pretty underwear; so I stitched ruffles and tucks, very fine tucks, and then added featherstitching. I was very proud of them, and I could hardly wait to see John. He came in at last, and as soon as I could I danced out in front of him.

'How do you like my handiwork?' I asked him, and he laughed until he had to hold his sides. I was surprised and even a little hurt. I'd spent hours on those drawers. But still he laughed. And finally, when he could talk, I found out why.

'You see, nobody had ever told me how to bleach out the lettering that was on every sack. I had tried boiling, but it had only turned the red letters to a delicate pink. 'Oh well,' I had told myself, 'the letters will all be lost in the folds.'

But they hadn't been; and on the side of me, in back, was plainly printed in large pink letters 'THE PRIDE' and on the other side 'OF TEXAS.'

Winifred Kupper, *The Golden Hoof*, 1945

25

A FRONTIER LOVE STORY

Colonel Albert C. Pelton, whose beautiful twenty thousand acre ranch is out toward the Rio Grande, near Laredo, has been the "Peter the Hermit" of Texas for years. He has believed that he held a divine commission to kill Apache Indians. Colonel Pelton came to Texas in 1844, a common soldier. By talent and courage, he rose to the rank of colonel, finally, in 1867, he commanded Fort McRae. That year he fell in love with a beautiful Spanish girl near Albequin, New Mexico. Her parents were wealthy and would not consent to their daughter going away from all her friends to live in a garrison. . . Finally, after two years of courtesy and devotion, Colonel Pelton won the consent of the beautiful Spanish girl and they were married.

Then commenced a honeymoon such as only lovers shut up in a beautiful flower environed fort can have. The lovely character of the beautiful bride won the hearts of all the soldiers of the fort, and she reigned a queen among the rough frontiersmen. One day, when the love of the soldier and his lovely wife was at its severest, the two accompanied by the young wife's mother and twenty soldiers, rode out to the hot springs, six miles from the fort, to take a bath. While in the bath, which is near the Rio Grande. . .a shower of Indian arrows fell around them, and a band of Apache Indians rushed down upon them. . . Several of the soldiers fell dead, pierced with poisoned arrows. This frightened the rest, who fled.

Another shower of arrows and the beautiful bride and her mother fell in the water, pierced by the cruel shafts of the Apache. With his wife dying before his eyes, Colonel Pelton leaped upon the bank, grabbed his rifle and killed the [Apache] leader. But the Apaches were too much [and he] was pierced with two poisoned arrows, so he swam the river and hid under a ledge. After the Apaches left, the Colonel made his way to Fort McRae. Here his wounds were dressed and he finally recovered, but only to live a blasted life—without love, without hope—with a vision of his beautiful wife . . .dying perpetually before his eyes.

After the death of his wife a change came over Colonel Pelton. He seemed to think that he had a sacred mission from heaven to avenge his young wife's death. . . He was always anxious to lead any and all expeditions against the Apaches. Whenever any of the other Indians were at war with the Apaches, Colonel Pelton would soon be at the head of the former. He defied the Indian arrows and courted death.

Once, with a band of the wildest desperadoes, he penetrated a hundred miles into Apache country [and] the Apaches fled, leaving their women and children behind.

It was then that there darted out of a lodge a white woman. "Spare the women," she cried, and then fainted to the ground. When the Colonel jumped from the saddle to lift up the woman he found that she was blind. "How came you here, woman, with these d____d Apaches?" he asked.

"I was wounded and captured," she said, "ten years ago. Take, oh take, me back again."

"Have you any relatives in Texas?" asked the Colonel.

"No; my father lives in Albequin. My husband, Colonel Pelton, and my mother, were killed by the Indians."

"Great God, Bella! Is it you, my wife?"

"Oh, Albert, I knew you would come!" exclaimed the poor wife, blindly reaching her hands to grasp her husband.

Of course, there was joy in the old ranch when Colonel Pelton got back with his wife. The Apaches had carried the woman away with them. The poison caused inflammation, which finally destroyed her eyesight.

San Antonio Daily Express, January 25, 1883

A DUMB HERO

In 1901, one of the most isolated districts in the United States was on the Texas-New Mexico line one hundred and fifty miles from a railroad. Four of us were employed in breaking horses on the old Block ranch, and on the Sunday in question, we saddled our broncs with no other thought than of another hard day's work. About 10 o'clock a ragged kid loped up on a horse which showed his place was drawing a wagon, and not being used as a saddle horse.

"Please, Mr. Cowboys," he said, "Ma is orful sick at our wagon, and pa sent me to ask one uf you to go to Plainview atter a doctor."

At that time in the west you acted first and asked questions afterwards. The fact that a sick woman probably lay dying at a lone camp was sufficient to cause action. Fifteen minutes later the saddle band was in the corral, and as I spread a loop for throwing I had already selected the horse for that life and death ride.

He was known as the B J Brownlow, an outlaw. Sired by a Kentucky stallion, crossed with a mustang mare, he possessed the speed and endurance of an antelope, the disposition of a hyena. Quickly saddled, and because I was the youngest and the lightest rider there, I was soon on my way.

After a wild spell of bucking this horse settled down into a half gallop, that had formerly carried him countless miles with the wild bunch over the same prairie he was now traversing. Finally I began to pull him down occasionally to catch his breath. Then on again in that tireless lope. The first stop was at Lazy S line camp thirty miles away. How thankful I was to draw near it for I, as well as the horse was beginning to feel the strain. Riding up to the dugout I found it deserted and no horses in sight. The next ranch was twenty-five miles farther on. Could he make it? I had ridden hard expecting a fresh mount there. Five minutes rest for him, two swallows of water, and I was off again. Lope! Lope! The miles fell behind. Sweat broke out all over the horse's head, and lathered his sides, but his wild spirit never flagged. He was game.

Five miles from the next ranch I saw the owner riding toward a gate where we would converge. I quickened up the speed although I could feel B J hitting the ground flat footed, the spring all gone from his muscles. One hundred yards from the gate he suddenly stopped, tried to go on, then with a scream which haunted me for many days, sprang into the air and fell dead.

Five minutes later a fresh rider was dashing to Plainview while I leisurely went to the camp to rest. The doctor arrived. The woman died, but her child lived. As I returned next day and passed the gate, I saw where the coyotes were working havoc on the remains of B J Brownlow, a dumb hero who gave his life for mankind.

Max Coleman of Lubbock, writing in the *Frontier Times*, December 1930

TEXAS EATS

Wild Mustang Green Grape Pie

Wild Mustang Green Grape Pie is a true treat from Texas past, and it is still enjoyed today by those of us who have access to a place where the delicate grapes can be picked. Grandma said that her mother made a cobbler with the grapes because a pie would not go around their large family of five boys and three girls. She said that the trick for a perfect pie was to pick the grapes at just the right time, while they were still a luscious green color and just before the seed formed.

3 cups green mustang grapes

1 1/2 cups sugar

3 tablespoons flour

3 tablespoons butter

Unbaked pastry for a 9-inch two-crust pie

1/4 cup melted butter

Sprinkling of sugar

Wash the grapes and put in a saucepan with just enough water to cover; bring to a slow boil. Combine the sugar and flour and add to the grapes when they begin to boil. Add butter and cook over medium heat, stirring gently, about 5 minutes, until the mixture begins to thicken. Pour into an unbaked 9-inch pie crust and top with a lattice crust. Brush the top crust with a little melted butter and a sprinkling of sugar, if desired. Bake at 400 degrees for 10 minutes. Reduce heat to 325 degrees and continue baking 20-30 minutes.

Candy Wagner & Sandra Marquez,
Cooking Texas Style, 1983

How to Make an Indian Bow and Arrow

[Indian] bows were usually made of bois d'arc, split out, and were about five feet long. The strings were made of a very strong sinew found in the buffalo, cattle and deer. These were dried and twisted. The arrows were made of dogwood, pointed with steel, and feathered with the wing feathers of turkeys, buzzards, or hawks. The grooves were cut lengthwise in the arrow into which the feathers were fitted. Places were opened up in the feathers for the sinews, the arrow was gripped in one hand, one end of the sinew was held in the teeth, while with the other hand the wrapping was done. When the feathers were securely wrapped, the edges were trimmed straight with a knife, making each side the same length This feathered end gave direction to the arrow and made it a dangerous weapon. With one well-directed discharge of the bow, a horse, a cow, or a buffalo might be killed. The arrows were carried in quivers made of calf or panther hides, each holding about 250, and were suspended over the shoulder by a strap. The warrior held his bow in his left hand, reached over his left shoulder with his right hand to secure his arrow. . . These could be shot with accuracy and rapidity.

Abilene Reporter, December 27, 1936

✪ ✪ ✪ ✪ ✪ ✪ ✪ ✪ ✪ ✪ ✪ ✪ ✪ ✪ ✪ ✪ ✪ ✪

"There is much work and hardship, rough fare, monotony and exposure connected with the [cattle] roundup, yet there are few men who do not look forward to it and back to it with pleasure "

Theodore Roosevelt,
Ranch Life and the Hunting Trail,
reprinted in 1978

It's Our Aggie Corps Upbringing

Nothing was regarded as a greater violation of established etiquette than for one who was going to drink not to invite all within a reasonable distance to partake, so the Texians, being entirely a military people, not only fought but drank in platoons.

Andrew Forest Muir, *Texas in 1837*

☙ TEXANESE ❧

Wear the bustle wrong

This takes some explaining. Once women wore large, bulky bustles, which were usually bone frameworks to expand the dress material. Bustles were worn in the rear and made women's hindquarters seem, well, extended. Bulky. Substantial. "Rump-sprung," as one early rancher described the effects of a bustle. So, whenever a cowboy saw a pregnant woman, she was said to be wearing her bustle wrong. Naturally, the phrase was extended to mean something done backward.

★ ★ ★ ★ ★ ★ ★ ★ ★ ★ ★ ★ ★ ★ ★ ★ ★

"The saucy schooner
off she go,
Merrily on to Texas ho!"

Sea chanty heard on New Orleans' dock, about 1840

A TEXAS CRIMINAL DISCUSSES THE MEANING OF LIFE

Texas badman Bill Longley was hanged October 11, 1878. Earlier, from jail he wrote philosophically of his life on the owlhoot trail and approaching execution

April 11, 1878

I take my pen in hand to let you know that I still float through the greater [illegible] of misery, destined to that inevitable doom that awaits me sooner or later, but,

"Let the wide world wag as it will,
I am still the same old rattling Bill."

Well, about eleven years ago I launched my boat upon that mighty river. . .without the least idea where it would lead me. Of course you are aware that when once one gets under good headway going down this mighty channel it is very hard to check up. I have found that this great river has but one landing place, from its head to its mouth: the name of that place is Reformationtown, and, after one passes Reformationtown there is no stopping place between him and eternity. No, none. But, O, how few there are who get off at this landing. . . !

I sometimes ask myself these questions: Is this world or this life only a dream? Will, all, then, be a universal blank, without a single prize? Oh! Certainly Not! Most undoubtedly there is a future. . . No ministers ever came near me, and I have never read the Bible a great deal, for I have spent my life, from a fifteen-year-old boy, in the wildest parts of the country, and in company with the most [illegible] men on earth. But with all, there has always been a spark of Christianity in my heart, and it has kept me from committing many evil deeds which I would have committed had I been void of that feeling. I have done enough, however, to ruin me; at least in this world, but I hope not in the world to come. . .I believe I could die a Christian if people would quit tantalizing me. I don't think I deserve to be abused as much, for I have never killed a man for money. It is true I have killed several men, but I always thought at the time that I had a good cause for doing so.

William Preston Longley

★ ★ ★ ★ ★ ★ ★ ★ ★ ★ ★ ★ ★ ★ ★ ★ ★ ★

The Drummer was in Sam Murray's saloon in Sheffield, Texas

. . . enjoying a quiet drink when a cowboy, wheeling his horse away from the bar, caused the critter to stomp on the drummer's foot. Immediately the drummer took his complaint to the bartender, who was Sam Murray himself. But there was no sympathy, much less compensation, forthcoming from Sam.

"What the hell you a-doin' in here afoot anyhow?" he asked.

Paul Patterson, *The Sunny Slopes of Long Ago*, 1966

THE FIRST TEXAS CHRISTMAS

Ninety-four years ago Texas celebrated its first Christmas. Religious services were held in the small settlements of the state, none of them at that time large enough to be regarded as cities. Some, indeed, were true "outposts of the wilderness." General Sam Houston, the idol of his fellow Texans, made a speech at Washington-on-the-Brazos, in which he said a republic could be founded only by a sober and industrious people. The hero of San Jacinto knew the virtue of sobriety, although in his sometimes turbulent and always picturesque career, he frequently forgot to practice it. . .

There was no prohibition law in Texas then, and after General Houston finished speaking a big party was held. Eggnog flowed freely and the revelers danced late. Simple presents were exchanged. . . Texas was farther away from the country's center of population then, because of poor transportation facilities, than Europe is now. Even if the toys were few and most of them handmade, the children and the young people had a good time. Christmas was celebrated mainly by eating, drinking and merrymaking. . .

The commentators say that Christmas of 1836 was very cold. Rains made the roads more impassable than they usually were and further contributed to the discomfort of travelers. Indoors, however, Texans gathered about roaring fires, sang, danced, ate wild turkeys and other fare and had a good time.

Transportation had improved somewhat in 1838, so that a Texan could get his favorite brand of liquor from New Orleans, Memphis, Nashville or some other distribut-ing point. Christmas day was observed quietly at Washington-on-the-Brazos. Christmas, 1839, was cold and rainy. Christmas supplies could now be obtained from New Orleans, Galveston or Indianola. In 1840, the French tricolor and the American flag were raised in front of the capitol of Texas, denoting that the infant [republic] had been recognized by France and the United States. In 1846, Texans rejoiced at the news that the United States had ratified the Texas annexation bill.

By Christmas, 1850, Texas had begun to put on airs in good earnest. Masque balls and confetti carnivals were the order of the day. . . Texans danced the square dance, the Virginia reel and other dances of the period. The official caller was an important functionary, and he often had as much liquor in his stomach as he and that useful organ could conveniently carry. Christmas trees were numerous. The young ladies and gentlemen wore dazzling costumes, the young men going in rather strongly for mustaches and whiskers.

And so Texas celebrated Christmas through the years when it was a young republic, when it was a younger member of the American sisterhood of states, through the trying period of the Civil War and reconstruction down to modern times. Texans have ever loved good cheer. They still love it.

Beaumont Enterprise, December 1930

★ ★ ★ ★ ★ ★ ★ ★ ★ ★ ★ ★ ★ ★ ★ ★ ★

FORMAL DRESS

It is rumored of one important sheepman of West Texas that he had a special pair of patent leather high-heeled boots made to wear with his tuxedo, simply because he cannot dance in anything but good cowboy boots.

Winifred Kupper, *The Golden Hoof*, 1945

*Y*esterday in San Antonio *the sun set as usual. . .*with no appearance of a storm. At 7:30 p.m. the heavens darkened, the wind commenced to blow from the north and the lightning became very brilliant. It continued thus until 8:30, when the wind freshened, the rain commenced to fall, and within 15 minutes it had increased to a hurricane, accompanied by the most fearful hail shower ever known.

Chunks of ice fell as large as a good-sized water pitcher, one weighing two and one-half pounds by actual weight. Every exposed glass towards the north of the city was dashed to pieces in an instant. Fronts of stores were opened, merchandise destroyed, houses blown down and men cut to shreds. Among the details reaching us, we learn of two men on a dray [freight wagon]—Mr. Louis, one of the party, was knocked off the dray and returned badly battered, and bleeding profusely, not knowing what had become of his companion and dray. . . .

Trees two feet through were twisted off like pipe-stems, and the hail dashed through tin roofs, leaving holes as clean as cannon balls would have done. A roof 40 feet long sailed off the Alamo and landed 200 yards away, in the center of Alamo Plaza.

Ten minutes after 9 p.m., the storm had subsided, the stars were shining beautifully, and the rattling of broken glass sounded in every part of the city. . .

We learn by telegraph that the hailstorm commenced eight miles this side of New Braunfels, reached only a short distance below our city, and extended from five to 25 miles in width, destroying everything over a region 30 miles from north to south and 10 to 20 miles from east to west.

San Antonio Express, May 20, 1868

★ ★

TEXAS' FIRST ANTI-FENCE-CUTTING LAW IN 1884

"Any person who shall willfully and wantonly cut, injure or destroy any fence or part of a fence. . . shall be confined in the penitentiary not less than one nor more than five years."

*W*hat's become of the punchers
we rode with long ago?
The hundreds and hundreds
of cowboys
We all of us used to know.

Traditional, attributed to
N. Howard Thorp, circa 1910

How to Cowboy Dance

A cowboy dance isn't the most beautiful thing on earth but it sure is lively; and sometimes when you get to watching the sets and the sashaying and the do-ci-do-ing, and listen to the strange shuffling rhythm which makes a square dance and is not possible to describe, along with the wild beckoning of the fiddle and the voice of the caller, then it is beautiful, in a way primitive expressions of happiness usually are.

Our ladies were lightfooted, even if they were the same ladies that stood over a wash-tub and a hot stove and could shoot down a coyote with one shot and no competition. They were pretty too—and they never got tired.

Jim Winslow's four-piece band (of Big Spring) was in great demand out here (in West Texas). They played all over the plains. When the band started out in Lubbock, which was one hundred and twenty-five miles away, on horseback, they let folks along the way know they were coming and stopped off at Gail and Tahoka and made merry in the best barns and stables or anywhere else they could find a place big enough to shake a foot in.

They stopped overnight and played for a dance in every town. There was some kind of mental telepathy accompanying their progress through the country, because there weren't any telephones and the mail hack was the only means of communication between towns; but whenever the Winslow Band got to a wide place in the road the cowboys were there in large numbers, together with a few well-chaperoned girls and some old folks who were not too particular with their feet and still had a dancing spark left in their make-up. . .

The square dances were still far and away the most popular, but waltzes were beginning to come in and the girls all swooned with joy when the fiddles struck up, "After the Ball Is Over." We danced schottische and many a lively polka. "Put Your Little Foot" was the best of all. Nothing is as pretty as a young girl in a wide lawn skirt, "putting her little foot."

The girls were outnumbered about five to one, so their popularity was legendary. Also their endurance. The men got to rest about four-fifths of the time but the girls danced every dance and the dances lasted all night— sometimes the next night, too. . .

The main reason the dances lasted all night was because it was a long time between dances and then, too, the durn roads were so bad, where there were any roads, and snakes and skunks made traveling by night kind of undesirable. So they shuffled all night long and when dawn began to come up over the prairies and it got light enough for the cowboys to get going, they unhobbled their horses, pulled off their boots and rested their feet and the horses carried them back to the ranch. . .

Shine Philips, Big Spring
The Casual Biography of a Prairie Town, 1942

GOING TO HEAVEN IN A PACKING CRATE

At a frontier [military] post, it was often impossible to get enough new lumber to make a coffin. When there was a death among officers or soldiers, often old packing boxes had to be brought into requisition. An officer died at a post in Texas, and nothing could be found for a coffin but some old commissary boxes, which were hastily put together and the poor fellow was carried to his last resting-place in a very rough one, on which was marked in great black letters, "200 lbs. bacon!"

Lydia Spencer Lane, *I Married A Soldier*, 1892

WEST TEXAS: A MIRACLE DRUG

[The Staked Plains of Texas] shall be the chosen land, perpetual sunshine shall kiss its trees and vines, and, having stored in luscious fruits and compressed into ruddy wine, will be sent to the four points of the compass to gladden the hearts of all mankind; and this shall be our sanitarium, a huge hospital where the afflicted of all lands will come and partake of Nature's own remedies. They will breathe the pure and bracing air, bask in the healing sunshine. Sickness shall be vanquished. The people shall die of age greatly prolonged.

David M. Emmons, *Garden in the Grasslands*, 1971

★ ★ ★ ★ ★ ★ ★ ★ ★ ★ ★ ★ ★ ★ ★ ★ ★ ★ ★ ★

A GRITTY LULLABY

. . .the northern panhandle of Texas . . . 'way up on the wild and windy plains, 3600 feet high, flat as a floor, bald as an eight ball, with nothin' in the world to stop that North Wind but a barb wire fence about a hundred mile north, and all of them barbs is turned the same way. . .where the oil flows, the wheat grows, the dust blows and the farmer owes.

"The Dustiest of the Dusty" by Woody Guthrie, excerpted from liner notes of a Victor album, 1940

✪ ✪ ✪ ✪ ✪ ✪ ✪ ✪ ✪ ✪ ✪ ✪ ✪ ✪ ✪ ✪ ✪ ✪ ✪

1857 TEXAS PRICES
$ $ $

Gingham cloth: 31 1/4 cents per yard
Silk velvet: 20 cents per yard
Sugar: 17 cents per pound
Tobacco: 38 cents per pound
Ladies' shoes: $1.75 per pair
Buckshot: 25 cents per pound
Whiskey: 15 cents per pint

ROUTE OF THE OLD CHISHOLM TRAIL

Beginning in San Antonio:

Through New Braunfels, next San Marcos, the trail crossing the San Marcos river four miles below the town.

Austin was the next town, the trail crossing the Colorado river some three miles below the Texas capital city.

From Austin, the drive was made to Georgetown and thence northward passing to the east of Salado and on to Belton.

The trail crossed the Leon River and wound its way Kansasward. . .and crossed the Brazos river to the right of Cleburne and stretched away to Fort Worth passing through what is now the eastern suburbs of that city and close to its then "Redlight District," which often was the scene of exciting, thrilling and tragic episodes.

After Fort Worth, the trail next touched Elizabeth and then Bolivar—two towns now only memories with the old trail drivers. It was at Bolivar that the trail forked and the greater number of herds were driven up the Elm through St. Joe in Montague county, a city made famous in trail days by the name of Justin, a cobbler who enjoyed the reputation of turning out the best cowboy boots along the long trail.

Red river was crossed after leaving St. Joe and the trail led through the Indian country encountering streams, including the Washita and Canadian until Kansas was reached at Caldwell.

In Kansas, the trail led to Solomon, Abilene and Ellsworth [where] the cowboy quickly forgot his weariness and trials and set himself to the full enjoyment of life according to his inclinations and appetites.

Remembered by old trail driver E.B. Baggett for the *Temple Telegram*, October 5, 1930; this routing possibly contains errors; in Fort Worth, for example, the trail passed to the west, not east.

THE FIRST RODEO

The first rodeo that was held for prize money in Northern Texas, was at Seymour, Baylor County, in July 1896. Those were halcyon days for the little town. In 1890-91 it bore the distinction of being the largest cattle shipping point in the United States. This first rodeo came into existence through the suggestion of Harry Dougherty, county clerk of King County. Noticing that the old settlers, soldiers, rangers, etc., had their reunions, he got together with a bunch of his colleagues and the result was "A Cowboy Reunion," as it was then called. The horses were "outlaws" from the big ranches and the open range; the steers were the wildest from the "breaks" of the Wichita.

One of the best of the "Old Guard," Emeline Gardenhire, of the U.S. Ranch. . .won first prize for broncho riding at the Seymour reunion. This consisted of the best suit of clothes and the biggest hat in town. "Montana Blizzard," the worst outlaw horse to be found in the country at that time, was the animal Gardenhire rode. Not only did he ride him, but he accomplished the feat with a loose silver dollar in the bottom of each stirrup, the dollar still being in place at the end of the ride. . .

Bill Parks, better known as "The Pitchfork Kid," of the Pitchfork outfit in King County, won first place in the roping contest, a fine saddle. . .

Seymour tried to make good her name in providing plenty of entertainment at this rodeo. Dozens of rude shacks were thrown up overnight as saloons, dance halls, and gambling dens, although, for the most part, the gambling was done out of doors—in the open, with the sky for the limit. Monte, faro, chuckaluck, Honest John, draw poker and craps occupied the time and pocket books of those present. Hundred-foot square box stalls were erected to be used as bars, each accommodating a dozen or more bartenders. A barbecue was held in connection with the affair, also, at which all manner of good things to eat and drink. Many a stray bullet punctured the walls and ceilings of the more permanent bars. "Old Red Eyes" was King of the carnival, and his subjects paid him lavish tribute.

Mary Daggett Lake, *Frontier Times*, May 1932

TEXAS PRAIRIE SUNSET

. . .When upon the wide prairie, night approaches the beholder, and the dazzling, golden rays of the sun begin to redden; and the mighty day god lays aside his piercing appearance and permits the eye of man to gaze upon him with impunity, then, indeed, the soul is filled with wonder at the sublimity of the scene. The gorgeous clouds form a rosy pathway for him to tread, as he walks downward into his bed of flowers and verdue. Around him float airy purple clouds, while beneath are others tinged with the richest of vermilion.

As he [the sun] sinks slowly down, he resembles a huge ball of fire falling amidst the grass of the prairie. When at length the sun is hid for the night, the fleecy clouds float for a few moments beneath the azure sky, and then disappear.

Then the bright silver stars come peeping forth, one after another, gladdening the eye with their twinkling light. Then comes up the full, round moon, attended by myriads more of bright stars, into the firmament already studded with these gems. Soon the light is sufficiently bright to enable the student to continue his labors by the moon's rays. He who is an admirer of the beauties of nature, can not look upon a scene like this unmoved. The wide prairie, which lies spread out on every side, is here and there relieved by a clump of trees, which serve to render the scene enchanting. Poets have often sung the beauty of Italian skies, but those who have seen both, pronounce ours equally beautiful. It does not appear to me possible that there can be a land more lovely than Texas.

William B. Dewees, Letters From an Early Settler of Texas To a Friend, 1852

TEXAS LOST ★ ★ ★ ★ ★ ★ ★ ★ ★ ★ ★ ★ ★ ★ ★
Whon, Texas

This is a case of early good intentions done in by a bad case of being Texan. This community in southeast Coleman County wanted to honor an esteemed local cowboy. He was Hispanic. When his name was suggested to the Post Office department, the local postmistress simply spelled his name as best she could—phonetically and in English.

Gene Autry, Texas

This never happened, but it almost did. Ol' Gene certainly wanted his name on his former hometown of Tioga, in Grayson County. In fact, he offered to buy the entire town if his name could be placed on it. Citizens declined. Our neighbor to the north was more receptive, and there is now a Gene Autry, Oklahoma, just east of I35 north of Ardmore. The settlement of Champion in Nolan County is not named for ol' Gene's horse.

Original St. Louis Day Coleslaw

The beautiful Gothic church in Castroville is the third St. Louis church on this site and is the result of work of a dedicated priest, Father Peter Richard. On August 25, 1870, special services were celebrated for the first time as the sun streamed through the beautiful stained-glass windows. Each year, on the Sunday closest to August 25, Castrovillians honor this memorable service with a festival that proves how dearly Alsatians love good food and drink. . . .

The townsfolk prepare a giant Alsatian sausage barbecue meal, and family recipes are featured at numerous food booths scattered throughout Koenig Park. If you can't be in Castroville for this memorable feast, you can share the original coleslaw. . . .

1 large head cabbage, shredded very fine

1 onion, chopped

1 green pepper, chopped

20 stuffed olives

1 cup sugar

Combine first four ingredients and pour sugar over vegetables. Let stand 15 minutes.

DRESSING:
1 cup white vinegar

1 tablespoon celery seed

1/2 cup salad oil

1 tablespoon salt

1 tablespoon prepared mustard

Combine ingredients and pour over vegetables. Serves 6-8.

Ann Ruff and Gail Drago,
Texas Historic Inns Cookbook, 1985

THE DEFENSE SPEECH OF SATANTA, A COMANCHE CHIEF, UPON BEING SENTENCED TO DEATH AT JACKSBORO, JULY 8, 1871

"I cannot speak with these things upon my wrists [holding up his arms to show the iron bracelets]; I am a squaw. Has anything been heard from the Great Father? I have never been so near the Tehannas [Texans] before. I look around me and see your braves, squaws and papooses, and I have said in my heart if I ever get back to my people I will never make war upon you. I have always been the friend of the white man, ever since I was so high [indicating by sign language the height of a boy]. My tribe has taunted me and called me a squaw because I have been the friend of the Tehannas. I am suffering now for the crimes of the Indians—of Satank and Lone Wolf and Kicking Bird and Big How and Fast Bear and Eagle Heart, and if you will let me go I will kill the three latter with my own hand. I did not kill the Tehannas. I came down to Pease river as a big medicine man to doctor the wounds of the braves. I am a big chief among my people, and have great influence among the warriors of my tribe— they know my voice and will hear my word. If you will let me go back to my people I will withdraw my warriors from Tehanna. I will take them all across Red River and that shall be the line between us and the pale-faces. I will wash out the spots of blood and make it a white land, and there shall be peace, and the Tehannas may plow and drive their oxen to the river; but if you kill me it will be a spark on the prairie—make big fire—burn heap.''

Satanta and other Indians attacked a wagon train from Fort Griffin May 18, 1871, killing six people. He was captured, brought to Jacksboro for trial and sentenced to death. The sentence was commuted by Governor Edmund Davis. Satanta committed suicide by leaping from the third floor of the prison at Huntsville.

THE INDIAN TRUTH

"Some people say that 50 years ago there were 500 [Alabama Indian] men, besides women and children. The last census showed some few over 250 in the tribe. Because of so little work in the village some worked at saw mills that are not far away. Tuberculosis and other diseases resulting from malnutrition are making inroads upon them, and if they are not given relief—not charity, but an opportunity to make an honest living for their families—the whole tribe will have died out in a few decades. Then the white man will sigh and say that civilization killed the Indian. The truth is that they have forced civilization on us, but have not taught us how to live in civilization.''

From a prize-winning essay on the condition of her tribe, the Alabamas, at their reservation outside Livingston, written by Miss Emily Sylvestine about 1932; her award was a one-year "high school" scholarship.

A PRAIRIE DOG PRIMER

The prairie dog is a species of marmot, with a head similar to a bull dog puppy, the incisors like those of a squirrel, body about the size of a common rabbit, and tail like that of a chip-squirrel. The immense numbers of these animals in one of their towns may be estimated from the fact that we passed ten miles through this town, and allowing it to extend the same distance in other directions, we have an area of one hundred square miles. When by estimating the burrows at seven feet apart, the usual distance, and six dogs to a hole, we have a population not to be exceeded by any city in the world. They are found all over the far western prairies, from Mexico to the northern limit of the states, and always select the sites of their towns upon the most elevated lands, where there is no water, sometimes none for many miles, but where grows a species of short wiry grass, upon which they feed. This had induced many to believe that they do not require water, and as no rains or dews fall during the summer months upon these elevated plains, the dogs never wander far from home, the conclusion is warranted that they require no water beyond what the grass affords. That they hibernate is evidenced from the fact that they lay up no store for the winter, and this grass dries up in the autumn. The Indians say that they may be seen, towards the last of October, busy with weeds and grass, stopping up every passage to their burrows, and if they reopen them again before spring, mild and pleasant weather is sure to follow. Usually, however, they never appear until settled weather in the spring, when they are about as lively as ever.

W.B. Parker, *Expedition Through Unexplored Texas in 1854,* 1856

JOHN STEINBECK EXPLAINS TEXAS

I've studied the Texas problem from many angles and for many years. And of course one of my truths is inevitably canceled by another. Outside their state I think Texans are a little frightened and very tender in their feelings, and these qualities cause boasting, arrogance, and noisy complacency, the outlets of shy children. At home Texans are none of these things. The ones I know are gracious, friendly, generous, and quiet. In New York we hear them so often bring up their treasured uniqueness. Texas is the only state that came into the Union by treaty. It retains the right to secede at will. We have heard them threaten to secede so often that I formed an enthusiastic organization—The American Friends for Texas Secession. This stops the subject cold. They want to be able to secede but they don't want anyone to want them to.

John Steinbeck,
Travels With Charley, 1962

TEXAS EATS

Prickly Pear Jelly

How are you going to get those prickly pears without being punctured like a tire in a sea of tacks, I don't know. It's hard. First off, I'd suggest you put on gloves. Not some silly flowery gardener's gloves, but some rawhide gloves. Second, I'd suggest you carry a pair of kitchen tongs to pop the fruits from the cactus. And don't wear tennis shoes, 'cause sure as you reach for a good one way in the middle of the plant, a spine will get your toe. Don't mention the rattlesnakes. They love cactus. And how can you tell which fruit to pick? You should pick a few which still have yellow or green streaks. Add them for the pectin so you'll have real jelly and not soup. Fruit ripens in early summer and stays good well into August.

Prickly pear cactus fruit

Water to cover

3/4 cup sugar per cup of juice

1 tbsp. lemon juice per cup of juice

When you get your gallon or so of prickly pears in the house, just keep your gloves on and, using the tongs, singe the spines off the fruit by holding them over the fire. You can do this with an electric range as well as you can a gas stove. It's the same principle Grandmother used in getting the pinfeathers off the chicken. But you must examine the pears carefully because some of the worse offenders look like tiny hairs, but they're sure get you. Once you've singed the fruit evenly, rub it with a paper towel and examine in a good strong light. This really isn't hard. Sometime I have stuck an ice pick in the fruit to twirl it over the fire. That seems to be quick. Only after you're sure all the spines are off should you take off those leather gloves. Now wash the fruit carefully, cut in chunks, barely cover with water, and simmer until the fruit begins to go to mush (about 20 minutes). Now pour pears and juice through a colander lined with a wet jelly bag (or an old clean sheet) and catch the juice in a deep, heavy pot. Don't twist the cloth if you want really clear pretty jelly. Measure juice.

Using no more than 3 cups of juice at a time, bring the juice rapidly to a boil and boil vigorously for 5 minutes. Skim foam off. Now add the sugar and lemon juice, and boil rapidly until a candy thermometer reads 222 degrees and until the jelly sheets off a silver spoon (Grandmother's way of testing jelly).

Skim off foam while jelly is cooking. What if the jelly reaches 222 degrees but when you try to sheet it off the spoon, it just drips? That means you don't have enough natural pectin. If this happens you can always throw in a box of pectin at the last minute.

If the jelly sheets nicely at 222 degrees, simply pour into hot sterilized jars and seal immediately with paraffin. Although I personally think this jelly is sort of flat-tasting, the color almost makes it worthwhile.

Hold a jar up to the light.

Doesn't that look like the bloom on a baby's cheek? Beautiful.

Linda West Eckhardt, *The Only Texas Cookbook*, 1981

WHY FATHER MULDOON GOT SOCKED IN 1830 TEXAS

An important personage was Padre Muldoon, not only in San Felipe, where he made his home, but throughout the colonies, he being the only authorized agent of Cupid east of San Antonio. The father made a tour of the colonies occasionally when in need of funds, tying the nuptial knot and pocketing the fees therefore, $25 being the modest sum for his services. But his visits were so much like an angel's, and his charges so much on the opposite extremity, that the colonists had recourse to a plan of their own, combining in itself the essential features of both marriage and divorce. . .

When a couple concluded to join their fortunes they forthwith repaired to the alcalde's office and had him draw up a bond to avail themselves of the priest's services whenever he came around; both parties signed the bond and went on their way as man and wife. The plan had this advantage, that if they changed their minds before the priest got around they had only to go together before the alcalde and demand the bond, which they tore to pieces and were free again.

Padre Muldoon was a bigoted old Irishman, with an unlimited capacity for drink. He found a congenial spirit in the person of "General" Walker, with whom he was one day doing the town. Stepping into Frank Adams' grocery just as the crowd was preparing to "lubricate," Frank politely invited the newcomers to join them. Old Padre Muldoon elevated his nose. "No, I never drink with any but gentlemen," said he. Adams promptly drew back and dealt the padre a blow between the eyes which had the effect of considerably modifying his ideas of gentility. . .

Padre Muldoon, who was no fool. . . apologized for his offensive language and accepted the proferred drink.

Noah Smithwick, *The Evolution of A State*, 1900

❂ ❂ ❂ ❂ ❂ ❂ ❂ ❂ ❂ ❂ ❂ ❂ ❂ ❂ ❂ ❂ ❂ ❂

HOGWALLERS IN EARLY DALLAS

I have closely watched the wonderful development of all Texas during the last fifty years. That far back Dallas had one two-story house, a frame building, near the court-house. In front of this prominent building stood a tall pole with a fork of two limbs at the top. Fastened in this fork was a bell with a rope attached. At meal times this bell was rung to announce to the public that a good hot meal was on the table in the Crutchfield Hotel, all you could eat for 25 cents.

[Then]the very best level or hogwallow lands sold for 57 cents to $5 an acre. The cost to fence forty acres with rails, our only fencing, was more than the price of 160 acres of land. A barrel of salt was worth two or three barrels of flour . . .

In those days the grasshoppers came. They kept the sun completely hidden for several days and the only clouds that we saw were dense clouds of grasshoppers.

The native grass on the prairies was knee high to up under one's arms and very thick, but the hoppers ate every leaf from the trees and much of the bark. Also all the corn, cotton and every vestige of vegetation there was to be seen. We had to fight them out of our houses, and keep all doors and windows closed to keep them from eating our bedding and everything else in the house.

From an interview with John Eddy Allen, in an undated issue of the *Dallas SemiWeekly Farm News*.

MARSHAL THOMPSON NOTCHES AN EAR

One day while Ben Thompson, the English-born gambler, was town marshal at Austin, Texas, he received a report that a certain cowboy had shot a bullet hole through the high hat of a visiting Easterner. Aware that this particular cowboy was trying to establish a reputation as a gunslinger, Thompson borrowed a plug hat from a friend and strolled quietly into the saloon where the cowboy was boasting of his prowess.

"I hear," Thompson said to him, "that you are shooting plug hats here today. Perhaps you would like to take a shot at mine."

Thompson then raised his revolver and shot a tiny piece off the cowboy's ear. "I meant," he said, "to hit your ear. Did I do it?"

The cowboy indignantly showed proof that his ear had been hit. "Well then," continued Thompson, "get out of here." He grasped the would-be gunman by the cartridge belt and hurled him out upon the street, ending whatever local reputation the cowboy might have acquired as a dangerous desperado.

Wayne Card, "The Role of the Cattle Trails," *Nebraska History,* 1958

COMANCHES 1; WHITE GUYS, ZIP

. . .[U]ntil 1875 the Comanches were the principal and most stubborn adversaries the Texans had. . . Despite crushing superiority in numbers and military might, the best that Texas and the United States could do was to defeat the Comanches and their allies by logistic strategy. When the Comanches' ponies and food supply gave out, they had to give up; they were not defeated in battle in the strict sense of the term.

William Wilmon Newcomb Jr., *The Indians of Texas,* 1961

★ ★ ★ ★ ★ ★ ★ ★ ★ ★ ★ ★ ★ ★ ★ ★ ★

POWER OF THE PRESS

It was in Limpia Canyon [near Fort Davis in West Texas] that the mail stage was attacked by Indians, who captured a bundle of illustrated newspapers. They opened the papers and looked at the pictures with fascination. They were still engrossed in the newspapers when avenging troops fell upon them. After that the Indians had a special belief in the power of the press. The newspapers were magic, and soldiers could tell just where to find their enemies if they were looking at the ensorcelling pictures.

Richard Dunlop, *Great Trails of the West,* 1971

VERY ANCIENT WEST TEXAS JOKE

Stranger to Lubbock rancher:
"Does the wind blow this way all the time?"
Lubbock rancher:
"Nope. Sometimes it blows the other way."

BIG FOOT WALLACE GETS HIS OWN INDIAN

Big Foot Wallace killed some Indians in his time and captured others whom he usually turned over to the authorities. But one time he came into Castroville with a captive and in no mood to give him up. He wanted to celebrate; he wanted to show off his Indian, so he took the redskin with him from saloon to saloon until he finally attained that glorious stage of happy recklessness that only a comfortably drunk man can experience. A county officer, deciding it was time for him to take a hand in the affair, approached Big Foot to take the Indian into custody, but old Foot objected vociferously.

"If you want you an Indian," he informed the officer, "you go out and catch you one; this one is mine and you can't have him." And he did not give up his Indian.

Grace Miller White, *Frontier Times*, April 1941

TEXAS LOST ★ ★ ★ ★ ★ ★ ★ ★
Yell Settlement, Texas

What more fitting name for a community whose leading citizen was a circuit-riding hellfire and damnation preacher named Mordecai Yell? The Very Reverend Yell and others arrived about 1885 northwest of San Marcos in Hays County. No trace today of the place.

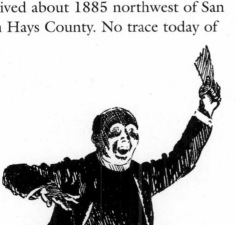

EARLY SALOON SHOOT-NOW, PAY-LATER PLANS

For several years [circa 1870s] Waco and Fort Worth were the wildest cowboy towns on the frontier. . .

Barrelhouse saloons occupied the best business stands. The bar was in front and the gambling department behind, with folding doors between.

It was the special thrill of drunken cowboys to ride into the saloons, shoot up the mirror and shoot holes in the heads of barrels of whisky and catch in glasses the amber liquor as it streamed out and then come around next day and pay the damages, leaving it to the saloon men to name the amount of the harm done, for they did not pretend to be conversant with the value of things.

Streams of wagons came and went, bringing in wool, buffalo, hides and meat and taking out supplies of various kinds. At all hours the streets and wagon yards were crowded. Great herds of cattle on the way to Kansas and the pastures and markets of the North crossed the Brazos at Waco. Later I made several trips as freighter to Lampasas and Brownwood, both wild towns, only on a somewhat smaller scale than Waco and Fort Worth. The people out that way could ride, rope and shoot straight. They were equally ready to settle any little dispute with you by shooting it out, or to give you anything they had if you seemed to need it worse than they did.

Onetime freighter S.H. Hall, remembering early Texas for the *Dallas News*, November 1930

*On the trail. . .*when the weather was good, the streams stayed in their beds, the cattle grazed in the cool of the morning and laid in the shade, lazily chewing their cuds in the heat of the day, while the outfit feasted on sourdough biscuits, good beef and straight black coffee, every son of a gun, from boss to horse wrangler, uncrossed his legs, got to his feet, licked off his knife blade and shut it down as he walked toward his horse, whistling or singing in that unmistakable way that said plainer than words that he wouldn't swap jobs with nobody.

That was trail life, all of it. And with the exception of an occasional fight, killing or Indian trouble for variation, it was all alike. No cowboy ever started on a drive expecting to get rich. He drew his wages at the trail's end and before he left town he had spent all of it, but enough to get home on. Sometimes he didn't have enough for that and had to borrow, or draw a month ahead, He knew that he was just a plain, everyday fool for staying on the job and cussed himself for it when time and place demanded that he should, but while he sometimes traded bosses and outfits, he never changed his job. I have never been able to account for it, even to this good day. Some of the old-timers say it was the wild freedom we had, others the tang of danger that always hung in the air, still others lay it to the feel of a galloping pony between your knees. I don't know which, or what, made it so fascinating. But I do know that it never leaves you.

Attributed to Bill Morgan in
Dallas SemiWeekly Farm News, circa 1930

There was something fascinating about the trail that I could never understand. It was a hard, hazardous life, the pay was not any too good, and an old trail hand would always swear that each trip was his last, but when the drive started the next season, you would find him on the trail again. They were a class of men by themselves, and had a code of honor all their own. They were good for their debts, they were good friends, and good sports, but as a rule they were not good men to fool with. I never knew one that did not have great respect for any nice women. They are about gone, and there will never be another class of men like them.

A.G. Mills, personal memoirs, 1933

★ ★ ★ ★ ★ ★ ★ ★ ★ ★ ★ ★ ★ ★ ★ ★ ★

ONE MEMORY OF MR. WILLIAM BONNEY AS SEEN IN OLD TASCOSA, TEXAS

[Billy the Kid] was only a boy. You'd never think he would kill anyone. He was good looking, with a smooth face, his hair was brown and wavy; his eyes were clear blue. The only thing about him that wasn't attractive, you might say, were two of his upper front teeth, one on each side, they were longer than the others and protruded a little. He was the best natured kid and had the most pleasant smile I most ever saw in a young man, and I've heard from men who saw him do it that he often wore that smile when he killed. At other times, so they told me, he had an awful look in his face when he killed a man. They say he had killed twenty-one men when Pat Garrett killed him, and the Kid was only 21 years old, so he killed a man for every year of his life.

I used to see the Kid often here and he and I became well acquainted. He was always heavily armed, but that wasn't unusual in those days; everyone went around with two heavy sixshooters sagging from his belt. The Kid always had a gang with him, bad men they were; but they behaved here. They had to; our boys wouldn't have stood for any funny business. We all knew of course, that Billy the Kid and his gang were bandits and horse and cattle thieves and killers, but they came here with horses to sell, and our cattlemen needed horses. We knew those horses had been stolen over in New Mexico, so we didn't care.

Attributed to Ms. Frenchy McCormick,
a onetime saloon faro dealer and
last resident of old Tascosa,
interviewed in the *Kansas City Star*,
December 1930

AND THEN THERE WERE NONE

The king of the stallions, the last of the wild horses in Western Texas, has a rope around his neck for the first time in his fifteen years of life.

The giant bay, the only animal in a 120-section pasture of J.H. Tippet in Culberson county, at the foot of El Capitan mountain, the highest peak in Texas, gave up after five cowboys had trailed him in relays for three days and night. Riding day and night, the cowboys finally got him.

The first time he was roped he bit the rope in two, but the second time it looped around his neck he gave up after a struggle that covered half the mountain side.

Frontier Times, January 1931

★ ★ ★ ★ ★ ★ ★ ★ ★ ★ ★ ★ ★ ★ ★ ★ ★ ★

I love old Texas, but barbed wire and locomotives have sure played hell with my country.

Attributed to Big Foot Wallace,
by Grace Miller White, in
Frontier Times, April 1941

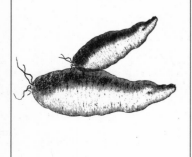
THE CONDENSED MILK DIRTY STORY

From those days when a cowboy first rode across Texas soil, he developed a strong, almost vehement, dislike for milk and cream. He didn't mind herding cattle, but he'd be damned if he would drink their milk. He didn't mind his breath smelling of whiskey and tobacco, but he certainly didn't want it smelling like that of a young calf.

In time, canned milk made its way to the plains. Women were delighted. Cowmen did not even like to talk about it. Charlie Russell once pulled a can of Eagle Brand from a cook's shelf and said, "I think it came from that bird. It's a cinch it never flowed from any animal with horns."

Carnation milk even advertised in stock newspapers that it would give a prize for the best jingle written praising the product. One ranching wife eagerly sat down and wrote:
Carnation milk, best in the lan',
Comes to the table in a little red can.

She gave it to a cowboy to mail, then waited with excitement to hear from the company. She heard. By letter they told her they could not use her poem because it was not fit to print.

The wife was at first angered, then bewildered, then confused. She called the cowhand and demanded an explanation. Had he altered her letter?

The cowboy grinned a shy, slow grin, then reddened under her boiling gaze. "Well, Ma'm," he said, "I read your poem an' figgered it was too short. I wanted to see y'u win that prize, so I figgered I could add a verse and make it better."

"Just what in creation did you write?"

"Oh, I jes' gave it a little more punch by makin' it read:
Carnation milk, best in the lan',
Comes to the table in a little red can.
No tits to pull, no hay to pitch,
Jes' punch a hole in the sonofabitch.

Traditional, retold in *Trail Boss's Cowboy Cookbook*, 1988

TEXAS GIVES BIRTH TO THE MARX BROTHERS

Somewhere during all this [about 1920], they stopped calling themselves "The Four Nightingales" and changed the name of the act to the "Marx Brothers & Co." Presumably this was to hide their identity, but essentially the act was the same. They were fooling no one, and by the time they pulled into a place called Nacogdoches, Texas, they were prepared for what could conceivably be a last ditch stand.

Their first performance in Nacogdoches was at a matinee. It was a real honkytonk kind of theater. "The audience was full of big ranchers in ten-gallon hats, and a few small ranchers in five-gallon hats," Father told me.

The first part of the performance went fairly well, but in the middle of the show the audience suddenly got up en masse and disappeared through the front exit. Investigation disclosed that the customers had gone outside to view a runaway mule.

My father and his brothers, though accustomed to insults, were enraged by this one. When the customers filed back into the theater, thirty minutes later, the Marx brothers were no longer interested in giving a good performance. All they wanted to do was get even with the audience, and the only way they knew how was to burlesque the kind of singing they had been doing so seriously.

This quickly evolved into a roughhouse comedy bit, with the Marxes, led by my father, flinging insults about Texas and its inhabitants to the audience as rapidly as they could think of them. . . .

My father is not very clear about the exact phraseology of some of these insults, but he does remember calling the Texans in the audience "damned Yankees" and throwing in a couple of lines that went something like:

> *Nacogdoches*
> *Is full of Roaches.*

And:

> *The Jackass*
> *Is the finest*
> *Flower of*
> *Tex-ass.*

. . .They were not looking for laughs; they fully expected to be tarred and feathered and run out of town on a rail. But instead the audience loved their clowning and greeted their insults and most tired jokes with uproarious laughter.

And so they were suddenly comedians, with their fame traveling all the way to Denison, Texas. The manager of the theater in Denison not only wanted to book them, but he offered to raise the salary for the whole act from fifty to seventy-five dollars a week.

"After that we were a pretty big hit everywhere else we played in Texas. I guess we could have stayed there indefinitely, but after we got ourselves reasonably solvent, we decided to go back to Chicago. After all, how long can anyone eat chili con carne?"

Arthur Marx, *Life With Groucho* 1954

★ ★ ★ ★ ★ ★ ★ ★ ★ ★ ★ ★ ★ ★ ★ ★ ★

"As I contemplate becoming a resident of Texas, I feel great solicitude about the nature of the population which will inhabit the country. . . The planters here have a most desperate opinion of the population there, originating I presume from such villains as have been driven from among them and who have taken shelter in that province."

Letter of January 31, 1829
from Thomas White of Louisiana
to Texas colonizer Stephen F. Austin

TEXAS POETICAL

Texas

Oh, a thirsty land of dust and sand
Is the Panhandle Plains of Texas
Where the coyotes howl and the
  panthers prowl
And the rattlesnakes strike and
  vex us!
And the people are strange who
  ride the range
For they went to the legislature
And voted the towns all "dry" by law
Tho the rivers were dry by nature.

Oh, the wonderful size of the
  enterprise
Of the State and the Folks of Texas;
Tho how they contrive to live and thrive
On the desert may perplex us!
For little they raise but milo maise
And cattle and cain and sand;
But when the grass is dry and the
  cows all die
They live by selling the land.

The land sharks bask in dusty pools
Where the lambs come down to
  the slaughter;
And they tell 'em the cows dried up
  on the range
Were drowned in the last high water.
'Tis the breeding place of a strong
  fit race
For the strenuous life that waits them
With their longhorned steers thru
  the long dry years
And the "dry" longwhiskered
  statesmen.

Attributed to a land speculator,
E.J. Palmer of St. Louis, after a visit
to the Texas Panhandle, about 1915.

THE UNSINGING COWBOY

I landed in San Antonio once badly in need of a job. I made contact with Ab Blocker, noted trail boss who was starting to the Red Cloud Agency with an Indian contract herd. I asked him for a job. He said, "I'm shorthanded but I've got to know whether you are eligible or not. Can you ride a pitching bronc? Can you rope a horse out of the remuda without throwing the loop around your own head? Are you good-natured? In case of stampede at night, would you drift along in front or circle the cattle to a mill?"

I said I certainly knew enough to mill them providing my night horse was fast enough to outrun the cattle.

"Well," he said, "that is fine. Just one more question: Can you sing?"

I said, "Yes," when I knew that I couldn't even call hogs, but I was sure needing a job.

Things went along pretty well for about twenty days. It seemed every time I was on guard the cattle would get up and low and mill around the bed ground. I was afraid the boss would find out the trouble sooner or later. One night I hadn't been out ten minutes when I commenced singing to them and most of them got up and commenced milling. I was doing my best singing when all at once the boss slipped up behind me. He was in a bad humor and said:

"Kid, you are fired. I thought you were causing this trouble. I thought you told me you could sing. It's a hell of a note that cattle can't stand your singing. You go back to camp and I'll finish your guard."

Ab was a good singer and in a few minutes the cattle commenced laying down.

Cowboy Jack Potter, quoted by Floyd Benjamin Street in
The Kaw: The Heart of a Nation, 1941

48

WHITES START THE INDIAN WAR IN FREDERICKSBURG

"It was the white man's fault," declared Mrs. G.O. Otte, an eyewitness of the Fredericksburg tragedy in 1852, "that there ever was trouble between the Indians and my people. . ."

She told how as a girl of five years of age she came over from Germany with her parents, who settled at Fredericksburg, then a frontier village of barely 300 inhabitants. Hundreds of Comanche Indians had their wigwams just one hundred yards from the Otte home on the eastern border of the little German village.

A close bond of friendship existed between the red man and the white settlers of the town. The white man exchanged his commodities for the hunting trophies of the Comanche. Their children played together.

Then came the tragedy. Mrs. Otte's oldest sister, Caroline, was employed in the home of the butcher of the town. One early morning in the summer of 1852, an Indian boy, about 13 years of age, is supposed to have come to the butcher's home holding one hand on his mouth and the other on his forehead, indicating that he was hungry and suffering from a headache. The butcher's wife was preparing food and medicine for the boy, when her husband entered the house. He is supposed to have grabbed for the boy, who with Indian alertness jumped behind the woman and begged her to protect him. She did not intervene. The boy was caught, his hands and feet securely tied, loaded on the butcher's wagon and taken to the Nimitz Hotel. . .

"A crowd gathered, among them my playmates and I," Mrs. Otte related. "After a lengthy conference, the mob moved about one half mile west of town. . . The boy was forced to gather wood for his own funeral pyre, built in the shade of a large pecan tree. Then the boy was fastened to the trunk of the tree. A number of men stepped forward and leveled their shotguns. . .

This savage action of the white man, according to Mrs. Otte, was watched by a small number of Indian warriors, who silently and solidly stood a little distance above the mob-scene.

"This bloody murder perpetrated by the white man upon an innocent Comanche boy, started all the trouble," continued Mrs. Otte. "Several weeks later the blood of the first white man, George Brode, was shed in revenge by the fierce warriors of the Comanches. Horses and cattle were stolen. The butcher was never killed."

Brady Sentinal, March 24, 1927

TWO TEXAS MURDERS

THE DEATH OF AN INDIAN EXPLAINED

Editor:

In your April number you published an article entitled "An Indian Boy Executed in Fredericksburg in 1852," taken from the *Brady Sentinel*, as related by Mrs. Otte. There are a number of errors in the article, which I shall attempt to correct.

My father and mother told me all about this affair, and, before I wrote this I asked an old man, who was one of the guards, all about it, and his version agrees with that of my father and mother. The Indian executed was not a boy thirteen years old, as stated in the article, but was a man some twenty-five years old. The name of the butcher mentioned in the article was Emil Wahrmund, Sr. His home was not in Fredericksburg at that time, but was eight miles south of the town, on Bear Creek.

The Indian came there one moonlight night, not with one hand over his mouth and the other on his forehead, but with the intention to steal Mr. Wahrmund's horses, and was prowling around the stable, which was locked, when scented by the dogs. These dogs immediately attacked him and when Mr. Wahrmund went to investigate, he found the Indian "treed" in a fence corner trying to keep the dogs off with a club. When he saw Mr. Wahrmund coming, he raised one of his hands, not to his forehead nor to his mouth, but as high above his head as he could get it.

Wahrmund took the Indian prisoner, took him to the house, and sent for help. Two men, John and Hanam Klein, came and guarded the Indian that night. The next morning they took him to Fredericksburg and delivered him to the sheriff. The sheriff told them to take him outside of the town and kill him.

They took him a mile beyond town and killed him, but not under a pecan tree, for there is no pecan tree there, never was, and probably never will be. The statement was made in the article that the Indian had to carry wood for his own funeral pyre. Positively not. They carried the wood themselves.

The Indian was executed because about a week before, the Indians had killed a man by the name of George Brode. It was also stated that the Indian was shot thirty times. He was shot one time and no more. The article makes it appear that the settlers were worse than the Indians.

[Signed] B. Markwordt, Harper, Texas

Frontier Times, June 1927

THE DEATH OF A SETTLER EXPLAINED

Jim Billings settled on Willow Creek, Gillespie county, Texas, in 1863, with his family. One day while he and his small son, John Billings, were out hunting their cows, some distance from their home, they were attacked by a band of Indians and the elder Billings was killed while the little boy escaped death only by a miracle.

John was about eleven years of age at the time, but he displayed a rare presence of mind and heroic fortitude that was remarkable for one of his tender years. Mr. Billings was armed with a rifle, and when they discovered the presence of the Indians the two were completely surrounded in an open space, with all chance of escape to a thicket cut off. The Indians began shooting at them, but before they killed him Mr. Billings shot one of the Indians. Little John, who was unhurt, resorted to a ruse, and fell to the ground as if shot, and lay perfectly still. They gathered around the fallen and for a time held high carnival, then all left but three of the redskins, who remained for a short while to make sure that their victims were dead. John dared not make the least movement for fear his ruse would be discovered.

Finally an Indian picked up a large stone and hit him a crushing blow in the face, knocking out several of his teeth and cutting a deep gash under his right eye. The pain from this almost was unbearable, but the boy bore it with fortitude and shammed death so effectively that the Indians went on, believing they had killed both father and son.

Before leaving, however, one of the Indians stooped over him and with a keen knife, cut his belt off and carried it away with him.

John lay flat on his back for a long time and then confident that the Indians had departed he went to a creek some distance away to quench a terrible thirst which seemed to be consuming him. Arriving at the creek he lay in the water a long time, in a semi-conscious state from the wound given him with the jagged stone.

[Neighbors] soon found little John in the creek, and he related to them what had happened and told them where they could find his father's body.

John Billings lived to be an old man, spending the later years of his life on a ranch near Mountain Home, in Kerr County.

Written for *Frontier Times*, by Miss Alice Nichols, June 1927

We enjoy a good scrap

Sooner or later, a fact is going to impress itself upon you. Throughout the West, wherever there was much fighting, there were Texians.

Frederick Bechdol, *Tales of the Old Timers* 1936

★ ★ ★ ★ ★ ★ ★ ★ ★

TABLE BLESSING ON THE RANGE

Yes, we'll come to the table
As long as we are able
An' eat ever damn thing
That seems sorta stable.

Cowboy blessing, circa 1880s

A *most delicious country; fertile, bountiful prairies covered with grass and flowers.*

Senator Thomas Benton, circa 1829

VIEWS OF TWO TEXAS BADMEN

John Wesley Hardin

Hardin killed men on the slightest provocation, and on no provocation at all. When he rode into a county, its inhabitants became panic-stricken: when he entered a town, its citizens were at his mercy and hastened to do his bidding. He killed anyone who thwarted him, and carved another notch on his gun. Criminals feared him as much as law-abiding citizens.

Hardin was a marvelous shot; and could shoot as well with his left as with his right hand. He could take a six-shooter in each hand, and with lightning rapidity, put all twelve bullets in a playing card at twenty

yards. He could handle his favorite weapon as a juggler handles painted balls; could twirl it around his finger by the trigger-guard so rapidly that it looked like a wheel; and at the word, shoot and hit the mark. He could fire a Winchester repeating rifle so rapidly that a continuous stream of fire came from the muzzle; and four or five empty shells from the ejector were in the air at the same time, falling from different heights to the ground.'

King Fisher

King Fisher and his followers stole the settlers' livestock; robbed their corn cribs; murdered those who opposed them.

Fisher was then [the late 1870s] about twenty-five years old, and a perfect specimen of frontier dandy. He was tall and exceedingly handsome. He wore the finest clothes procurable, and of the picturesque, dime-novel type. His white, broad-brimmed sombrero was ornamented with gold and silver lace, and had a golden snake for a band. His Mexican short jacket of fine buckskin, was heavily embroidered with gold. His sheer, expensive shirt was worn open at the throat, with a silk handkerchief knotted about its wide collar. A crimson silk sash was wound about his waist. His *chaperejos*, or "chaps," were made of a royal Bengal tiger, ornamented down the seams with gold fringe. The tigerskin had been procured at a circus in Northern Texas, where the desperado and his men—because he fancied the hide—captured the circus and killed the tiger. He wore high-heel boots of costly leather, and silver spurs ornamented with little silver bells. He rode the best horses he could steal in Texas and Mexico.

N.W. Jennings, *A Texas Ranger*, 1930

DREW BARRYMORE'S GREAT-GREAT-GRANDFATHER GETS SHOT IN EAST TEXAS

In the winter of 1878 there came through Marshall from New York a company of prominent young Thespians, who were just beginning to win their laurels in the theatrical world. The company was headed by that well known actor, Mr. John Drew—suave and witty—supported by the accomplished young actress, Miss May Cummings, and the dashing and handsome young matinee idol, Maurice Barrymore, father of Miss Ethel, Lionel and John Barrymore. On the fateful night. . .they repaired to the Texas & Pacific depot to take the midnight train out. . .

Jim Currie was of a prominent and well known Southern family, schooled and educated in the customs and traditions of his illustrious ancestors. He was addicted to the use of liquor and. . .on that eventful winter's night he was around the depot, and was what is commonly known in jargon as "three sheets in the wind." [Currie made] some drunken and laughing remark which appeared to be addressed to the theatrical party. Actor Ben Porter got up from his seat and said something about being unarmed, but that he would defend a lady from insult.

At this remark Currie jerked out his big smoke wagon and the shooting commenced. Porter staggered and tumbled over dead. By this time the handsome and debonair Maurice Barrymore was on his feet. [He glanced] at Ben Porter, whose life blood was by this time staining the floor. His eyes snapped like electric sparks, as he pushed Miss Cummings behind him and faced Currie. He must have known that he did not have a chance in ten thousand as he stood in front of Currie, who was inflamed by liquor and apparently either with the lust to kill or was just drunk and excited enough not to realize the seriousness of the situation. There was another shot and Barrymore, with a bullet through the shoulder, staggered around and collapsed on the floor. The room was partly filled with the fumes of black powder as Currie put up his gun, and taking hold of Miss Cummings, jollied her around with a drunken air of braggardism.

Then came a potpourri of excitement and Currie was disarmed by deputy sheriff Arch Adams, who placed him in jail. Mr. Barrymore was taken in charge by Drs. B.F. Eads and John H. Pope, railroad surgeons, and they pulled him through. Miss Cummings remained and nursed him during his convalescence, and in due time they returned to New York City. . .

Written for *Frontier Times* by
Clifton Seymour, January 28, 1927

★ ★ ★ ★ ★ ★ ★ ★ ★ ★ ★ ★ ★ ★ ★ ★ ★

A STAGECOACH HOLDUP IN 1879

When we got to Pegleg Station on the San Saba River, a fellow rode out and threw his gun down on the driver. The driver kept his hands lifted while the robber unhitched the team and ordered us from the coach. Four drummers, a young woman and I made up the passengers. He searched the drummers, but handed back the lady's jewelry, saying he didn't rob women. He looked at my cowboy outfit and said "Go on, you ain't got a damned thing."

Remembered by Sam Moore,
in *Frontier Times*, April 1937

How to Make Indian Smoke Signals

The Indians generally made their arrangements to start with their stolen horses within a day or two of the full moon and we always knew when to look for them. They seldom molested any of the citizens until they were ready to leave with their [stolen] horses and then they killed every person they saw if they could outrun or catch them.

A week or two before making their drives they would divide up into small squads, six or eight together, each one taking a route to spy out the country and find were the horses were located. They traveled in the open country during the night and located themselves on the mountains and high peaks in the day time from whence they could overlook the country and see where the horses were feeding.

They had signals by which each squad could tell where the others were, provided it was a clear still evening. They always gave their signals just at sunset. It was done by taking a cow hide and closing it together in the shape of a funnel, making one end as large as the hide would permit, and the other about eight inches in diameter, then piling up a lot of loose, dry grass, setting it on fire and then putting the hide over it with the big end down.

The burning grass forced the smoke through the small end of the hide with such force that it would shoot up in the air for a long distance and could be seen for many miles. Each squad gives the same signal and by that means each knows where the other is and, when their appointed time comes, and each one has meantime stolen a good horse to ride, they all start out at the same time, gather up the horses they have located and all meet with their herds of stolen horses at a place previously agreed upon.

We could always tell from the smoke signals when Indians were in the country. I have often stood on the public square in Gatesville and seen three or four smoke signals in different directions within a few minutes of each other. This was a sure indication that the Indians were preparing to make a drive on or about the full moon, and it was sufficient warning to those who were acquainted with the Indian tactics to keep a sharp look out about that time and not to expose themselves by careless traveling over the country—as many did, and thereby lost their lives.

From a speech by J.H. Crisman, Old Settlers Reunion, Belton, September 14, 1903

THE LADDER THIEF OF COLEMAN COUNTY

Colonel Perry, the biggest merchant in [Coleman, about 1880], was building the first big two story rock building in town, and had the upper story floored, the windows all in, and a temporary stairway, or rather a ladder, on the outside to enter the upper floor. There were a lot of cowmen and cowpunchers in town, and they decided to stage a big dance on the second floor of this new building. Everybody was invited and people came from great distances around. They had everything to eat and drink, the hall was crowded and everything was going fine. Late in the evening a boy by the name of Jack Mills misbehaved in some way and in putting him out he was treated rather roughly, which of course made the boy sore. He got his horse and rope, rode up to the building, tied his rope to the ladder and dragged it out on the prairie, leaving the crowd of two hundred people or more in the upper story of the building with no way to get down. It was late, and everybody in town who had not gone to the dance was asleep. Finally, about daylight we got help from outside and soon had a temporary stairway arranged.

A.G. Mills, *personal memoirs*, 1933

COMING TO TEXAS IN 1845

I had to wait nearly a week [in New Orleans] before I caught a boat going up Red River. It not only went up Red River but made its way through Soda and Caddo Lakes into Texas to a landing then and now called Jefferson. There were a hundred and thirty-odd passengers aboard.

This was the second boat that made its way to Jefferson. A majority of the passengers, like myself, were going to Texas. Many of them had their guns with them and put in much time shooting alligators on Red River and the lakes. We had eaten all the provisions on board and might have gone hungry had we not struck an Indian camp, on the bank of the river just before we entered the lakes, that furnished the captain with wild game.

Upon arriving at Jefferson, the captain notified us that we would have to look out for our own breakfast, as we had eaten all the rations on board. Going ashore next morning, I inquired where to get my breakfast. I was pointed to where smoke was coming up out of the brush nearly two hundred yards distant. In company with a young Tennessean I made my way through the brush to the smoke where a man served us with meat, bread, and black coffee, using a very large pine log for a table. This was my first meal on Texas soil.

There were several houses under construction but there was only one finished. It was a log cabin built without a nail in it. It was covered with split boards and they were weighted down and held in place by small logs on top of them. It had a puncheon floor and a stick and mud chimney.

Buck Barry, *Texas Ranger and Frontiersman*, 1932

The Texas Rangers Arrive in Mexico City

A regiment of Texas Rangers commanded by Jack Hays fought in the War with Mexico in 1847. The Rangers took great pride in not being confused with regular soldiers. Here's how two newspaper correspondents described the Rangers' arrival in Mexico City.

1. "There arrived here recently the greatest American curiosities that have as yet entered the City of the Aztecs They were the observed of all observers, and excited as much lively interest as if President Polk and the American Congress had suddenly set themselves down in front of the Palace, to organize a government and laws for the people of this blighted land. Crowds of men flocked to see them (however always keeping at a respectful distance) and women, affrighted, rushed from the balconies of their houses. Perhaps you would like to know whom these terrific beings are. Why, they are nothing more or less than Jack Hays and his Texas Rangers, with their old-fashioned maple stock rifles lying across their saddles, the butts of two large pistols sticking out of the holsters, and a pair of Colt's six-shooters belted around their waists, making only fifteen shots to the man. . .

"The Mexicans believe them to be a sort of semi-civilized, half man, half devil, with a slight mixture of lion and the snapping turtle, and have a more holy horror of them than they have of the evil saint himself. We have several times been asked by some of the inhabitants if the Texans will be allowed to go into the streets, without a guard over them. It is really surprising that men with such a reputation should be among the very best disciplined troops in our army, and not disposed to commit outrages or create disturbances in any way."

2. "They rode, some sideways, some upright, some by the reverse flank, some faced to the rear, some on horses, some on asses, some on mustangs, some on mules. On they came, rag, tag and bobtail, pell-mell, helterskelter; the head of one covered with a slouched hat, that of another with a tower cocked hat, a third bareheaded, while twenty others had caps made of the skins of every variety of wild and tame beasts: the dog, the cat, the bear, the coon, the wild cat, and many others, had for this purpose all fallen sacrifice, and each cap had a tail hanging to it, and the very tail, too, I am keen to swear, that belonged to the original owner of the hide.

"A nobler set of fellows than those same Texan tatterdemalions never unsheathed a sword in their country's cause, or offered up their lives on their country's altar. Young, vigorous, kind, generous, and brave, they purposely dressed themselves in this garb, to prove to the world at a glance that they were neither regulars nor volunteers, but Texas Rangers, as free and unrestrained as the air they breathe, or the deer in their own wild woods."

Frontier Times, March 1927

★ ★ ★ ★ ★ ★ ★ ★ ★ ★ ★ ★ ★ ★ ★ ★

A GENERAL LAMENTS TEXAS MANNERS

"On the day of battle I am glad to have Texas soldiers with me for they are brave and gallant, but I never want to see them before or after, because they are too hard to control."

General Zachary Taylor,
during the war with Mexico,
September 1846

VIEW OF AUSTIN IN 1857

Austin has a fine situation upon the left bank of the Colorado. Had it not been the capital of the state, and a sort of bourn to which we had looked forward for a temporary rest, it would still have struck us as the pleasantest place we had seen in Texas. It reminds one somewhat of Washington; Washington, en petit, seen through a reversed glass. The Capitol—a really imposing building of soft cream limestone, nearly completed at the time of our visit, and already occupied—stands prominent upon a hill, toward which, nearly all the town rises. From it a broad avenue stretches to the river, lined by the principal buildings and stores. These are of various materials and styles, from quarried stone to the logs of the first settlers. Off the avenue, are scattered cottages and one or two pretty dwellings. They are altogether smaller in number and meaner in appearance than a stranger would anticipate. The capital was fixed, in fact, upon a thinly-settled frontier, at a point the speculative, rather than the actual, centre of the state. There is a very remarkable number of drinking and gambling shops, but not one bookstore. The druggist, who keeps a small stock of books, sold us, at one dollar, giving his word that its cost was seventy-five cents to himself, a copy of "Eagle Pass" (one of Putnam's Semi-Monthly Library), the price of which, elsewhere is forty cents. The population, at the census of 1850, was 629; the estimate, when we were there, 3,000; a large one, we thought. The country around the town is rolling and picturesque, with many agreeable views of distant hills and a pleasant sprinkling of wood over prairie slopes.

Frederick Law Olmsted, *A Journey Through Texas*, 1869

ARTISTIC TEXAS

Nature appears here more than any where else I have seen, like a landscape-painter, composing a picture with the most simple yet refined taste.

Julius Frobel,
*Seven Years' Travel in Central America,
Northern Mexico, and the Far West
of the United States*, 1859;
the author, a German, was writing of
Texas' Davis Mountains region

Big Foot Wallace Fights an Indian

"I tell you, boys, I often see that Indian now in my dreams, especially after eating a hearty supper of bear meat and honey, grappling me by the throat with left hand, the gleaming butcher knife raised high in his right hand, and two eyes blazing down at me like a panther's in the dark.

"It is astonishing how fast a man can think under such circumstances. I looked upon the blue sky, and bright sun overhead. Then thought of mother as I remembered her when a little boy, the old home, apple orchard, and creek where I used to go swimming. All these, and many more thoughts, flashed through my mind in the little time [the Indian's] knife was gleaming over my breast.

"Suddenly, the Indian quivered, while on top of me, gave a yell, and down went the knife with a force that buried it to the hilt in the earth at my side.

"The last time I threw down the Indian [I had knifed him, and] a deep gash was cut in his forehead by a sharp-pointed rock, and blood running down his eyes from this wound so blinded him that he struck wildly with his butcher knife, the blade missing me about half an inch. I fully expected him to repeat the blow, but he lay still and made no effort to withdraw the knife from the ground. I looked at his eyes; they were set hard and fast, but there was a devilish sort of grin about his mouth as if he had died in the belief he had sent me before him to the happy hunting grounds.

"I threw his body off of me and got up weak and trembling. My knife had gone to his heart. I looked at the dead Indian for a while, lying there so still, and said to myself: 'Well, red warrior, you made a good fight, and if luck had not gone against you, you would have been where I am and I would have been where you are. Now I shall do for you what I never did for an Indian before—I am going to give you a decent Christian burial.

"So, I laid his rifle beside him, according to Indian custom, that it might be handy when he got to the happy hunting grounds, and gathered pieces of rock from the canyon, piling them around and over his body, until it was completely covered and safe from attacks of coyotes or other wild animals. There I left him at rest in his crude and lonely grave, a foe worthy of any man's steel. This is a true account of my fight with the big Indian in the canyon."

J.C. Duval, *The Adventures of Big Foot Wallace*, 1878

★ ★ ★ ★ ★ ★ ★ ★ ★ ★ ★ ★ ★ ★ ★ ★ ★

Lone Star Holler: The Why

"Of a sudden they stopped and gave a series of wild, bloodcurdling yells. . . The men on the great silent plains feel sometimes that they must let out their voices with all their power, just to break the monotony of a seemingly limitless prairie. . .We had a fashion of yelling like wild Indians at times, for nothing at all except to give vent to our exuberant spirits, born of the free, big life of the prairies."

Napoleon Jennings, describing the famous "Texas yell" in *A Texas Ranger*, 1899

ONE SHOTGUN, ONE RANGER

"My time just had not come."

That's the way [Texas Ranger] Captain John H. Rogers explains why he was able to walk into the muzzle of a double-barrel shotgun in the hands of a desperado who had it leveled at him and cocked, threatening to shoot if the ranger captain took another step.

It was at Cotulla in the early days. A saloonkeeper had been in the habit of shooting up the town and doing as he pleased. He resented the intrusion of the rangers.

Rogers' company had been there but a short time when the man got drunk, took several shots at another man who was riding away from the saloon, shot up the town and then defied arrest.

The saloonkeeper loaded a double-barrel shotgun with buckshot, cocked both barrels and said he would kill anybody who tried to arrest him.

"I looked in the door," said Captain Rogers, "and saw him with his gun to his shoulder. He had it leveled on me and both barrels cocked. My first thought was that maybe I had best not try to go in the front way.

"I naturally figured that he might shoot and that I had better try to get in the back way. But then I realized that such a step would be showing weakness and that it might cause trouble. There was but one thing to do and that was go in and get him right then and there. He had been getting by with his gun play too much and it would not do to let him think he had anybody bluffed."

Old rangers tell the rest of the story. "Praying" John Rogers walked right in to the muzzle of the gun that was leveled at his head and told the "bad man" he knew better than to shoot. "You have been getting by with this stuff too long. You'll have to cut it out," the captain was saying as he walked straight to the bar behind which the man had fortified himself. Captain Rogers then caught the gun by the barrel, raised it away from his head and caught the man by the collar. Come out of here—come with me," he commanded and the fact that Captain Rogers is living today proves that the gunman "came out."

San Antonio Light, September 10, 1925

TEXAS EATS

Pit BBQ for 600 People

The Pit:

With backhoe dig pit 6 ft. deep and 12 ft. long. One cattle truck load of mountain mahogany, oak or any of the harder woods. Must be dry. Feed the load of wood into the pit in three hours. Allow 2 1/2 hours to burn down to coals. Level coals with a metal rake. This makes about two and one half feet of coals.

The Meat:

Use 400 lbs. of roasts, rolled chuck or rump. Each should weigh about 15 lbs. Place 2 or 3 cloves of garlic in each roast, or put three peeled onions in each bundle. Cover meat with mixture of barbecue sauce and sugar cane. Wrap two roasts in cheese cloth. Use the tubular type used to wrap deer after it has been skinned. Wrap this in aluminum foil. Wrap in wet burlap. Tie with iron wire, making a loop on top of bundle to hook into in lowering and raising beef from the pit. Place a little sand with shovel under each bundle, on the coals. Be quick placing beef on coals and covering it up. Across top of pit place steel fence posts every two feet. Cover this with steel sheeting. Cover airtight with dirt. Cook 17 to 18 hours.

The Sauce:

6 gals. tomato sauce

20 lbs. onions, ground fine

1 bottle Worcestershire sauce

1 qt. molasses

2 tbsp. dry mustard

Cumin

Add vinegar and brown sugar until you get a sweet and sour taste. Start with 10 c. of brown sugar. Then add vinegar slowly. Simmer eight hours. You have lots of time to get the sweet and sour just right. Make barely warm with a little red pepper.

Trail Boss' Cowboy Cookbook,1988

THREE TEXAS NICKNAMES

. . .We set out for El Paso, and on the second or third day were met by a man who told us with great vociferation how the Indians had run off fifty head of his cattle from Eagle Springs. . . His nickname was "Talking" Campbell. In those early days of Texas [about 1854], men were named from some personal peculiarity, and we had then living "Big Foot" Wallace, a tremendous good-natured fellow from Rockbridge county, Virginia. On my first introduction to him I could not perceive any unusual size of his feet, and was informed that he acquired his cognomen honestly in battle, having slain a famous Indian chief known as "Big Foot." Then there was "Deaf" Smith, who once, when General [Sam] Houston ordered his army to lie down that they might be the better protected from the Mexican cannon, looked around him, and seeing the smoke of the Mexican guns and all his comrades prone upon the ground, did not tarry there a moment longer, but, turning, fled and reported all killed but himself. It was said that for years "Deaf" Smith was engaged in single combats because of this experience in his first great battle. Few men dared to mention San Jacinto or Sam Houston in his presence.

Then there was "Stuttering" Lane, a capital good fellow from San Antonio, who had many funny jokes, upon himself suggested by his infirmity. When asked why a certain lady did not marry him after promising to do so, he stammered out that she was going to marry him, till a certain "damn-fool-busy-body" told her he stuttered!

Lieutenant Dabney Maury, *Recollections of a Virginian*, 1894

✪ ✪ ✪ ✪ ✪ ✪ ✪ ✪ ✪ ✪ ✪ ✪ ✪ ✪ ✪ ✪ ✪ ✪ ✪ ✪

A LADY LAMENTS

I am not married yet and no prospects for it, for I should be afraid to select a man in Texas to marry unless I had known all about him before he came here, for I should be sure he had done something and been run off.

Miss Kitty King, in a letter from Fort Worth,
circa 1860

PECK SHARP WINS A PRISE

Sanantonio tex
June 18th, 1941

Old friend Al:

Inclosed you will find three dollars [I owe you], thought I had better send it in before Hitler came over here and took it away from me. . .

They hed the old trail convention here last week and I won first prise. Each man in the contest was to tell three old time stories, and after I had told two they gave me the Prise. Each storie had to be a true one about things that happened over fifty years ago, the stories that I told Happened over sixty years ago.

In dark valley in Pallo Pinto county I was punching cattle for old dock Simmons and their was a big Roan cow that ranged on lone mountain with horns as sharp as needles, and she would come down off lone mountain of a night and hook some of docks range cattle.

He offered a reward to any of his cowboys that would drive her into his correll or bring in a piece of her. There was many a cowhand tried to rope her but she stayed in the cedar breaks on lone mountain and none of the boys could rope her, so one Sunday me and an other fellow named Craig went up the pass on lone mountain to round up this Roan cow.

We hadn't rode very far when we seen the sedars russel and shure enough it was her. I told Craig not to let her go down the pass and I would rope her so away we went every—time we hit a little opening I swung my rope but it would hit a sedar and she kept going. . .

their was a presipis about two Hundred feet strait down and she was heading for it, and me and my bronk right at her heels. She ran right to the edge of the cliff and just as she was going over I grabbed her by the tale and took a couple hiches around my saddle horn and their she was hanging over the cliff, and my horse just hanging on with his hind legs, it looked bad for me and my bronk but I thought of my knife and cut her tale off and over she went and her old bones are still laying at the foot of that cliff today.

I took the tale into mr. Simmons and he gave me the reward.

The other favor I done Dock. There was an old burrow [burro] that had been hanging round his Corrells for years and was an awful pest, always in the way. Dock didn't want to kill him but wanted to get rid of him so he left it up to me to get rid of him.

Their was a wild bull, a big red fellow that came down on the range and whiped the other bulls and raised plenty of trouble so me and my pal cowboy Craig roped him one day and brought him in and got a stout rawhide rope and hitched the bull and the burrow together. Then we drove them up the pass on lone mountain.

In about a week some of the cow hands were on long mountain and saw that burrow standing on the edge of the Presipis with his head down and his feet stretched out in front of him, and when they rode up to him their was a big red bull hanging over the cliff, the way the ground was tore up looked like he had held him for two or three days.

One of the boys cut the rope and down went the bull and his bones are with the old Roan cow today to prove my story, and the burrow came back to the Correll and is a pest around their yet.

Best to all old Pals.

J. Peck Sharp
P.S. You can always tell a chopper by his chips

PEGLEG TELLS A STORY

All old time printers and telegraphers of the '80s remember "Peg," for he was a remarkable character, never to be forgotten . . .He had lost one of his legs in a railroad accident, having gone to sleep and fallen off the brakebeam, or something like that. . . The leg was really a fine one and "Peg" could, and did, get from $10 to $15 on it in any pawnshop. . .He was a great talker, and when only half-loaded, was very amusing. He told some good stories, too. I remember one in particular. . .

"Gentlemen," said he, "you can talk about your hot towns as much as you want to, but Santone takes the cake. I was out there last winter and I had the time of my life. There was a big variety show going on down on one of the plazas and, of course, I went to see it. . . The show was nearly over when a drunken cowboy came in. He had two big guns strapped round his waist and a Bowie knife that looked like a young sword . . .He swaggered about and the show had to stop for a few minutes [and then]. . . catching sight of the boxes on the edge of the stage, he made for one. Everybody seemed to be afraid of him and tried to quiet and pacify him. . .

"A fellow on the stage began to sing. The cowboy promptly ordered him to stop. The fellow paid no attention, but went on singing. . . Finally the singer got mad and, advancing to the front of the stage, asked if there was not an officer in the house to take the drunken nuisance out and lock him up. There was no response. . .[so the singer] advanced to the side of the stage and began climbing to the box. [The cowboy] reached out and dragged him into the box. They dropped to the floor in a clinch, but as they fell I saw the cowboy had his knife in his hand. . . Then I saw them rise, the cowboy holding the singer by the back of the neck. He rammed him face foremost against the wall and rammed that big knife through him twice and then, slamming it plumb through him between the shoulders, he left it sticking in his body and, picking him up, hurled him out of the box to the stage below.

"It was all over in a minute and there was the biggest stampede you ever saw. The whole audience made for the door in one solid mass, and I was working well in the lead, in spite of having only one good leg to work with. When I struck the sidewalk. . .I saw a policeman and rushed to him: I said, 'You had better go down yonder, a cowboy just murdered a man in the theater down there.' He looked at me and just grinned. 'That's all right,' said he. 'They been killing that same man for two nights now. It's part of the show.'

"Next night I went back to enjoy the fun of seeing the stampede, now that I knew it was part of the show. I got a seat near the end of a row. . .and there is where I was a fool. The cowboy came in and went through the same performance. There was the same stampede, too. . .[and] a big Dutchman near me stampeded at the first flash of the knife and took the whole tier of seats with him. In the rush they got my leg, the broomstick one, jammed in the seat and broke it square off. Then they walked all over me and I never saw a thing. When the dust settled they found me all spraddled out on the floor. The proprietor acted pretty square. He set 'em up two or three times, sent me home in a hack and next morning early they had a carpenter come 'round and fix my stem, and that night I left for El Paso. Santone was too strenuous for me."

S.O. Young, *El Paso Times*, circa 1923

We had been ordered back to Fort Worth

. . .[but] I wanted to stay at Camp Colorado [Coleman County] as my term would soon be up and I intended to homestead a piece of land. I, with three men, went down the creek two or three hundred yards and began a game of poker. Just as I was upon the point of demanding a "showdown" I looked up and saw an Indian jump behind a tree. The others wanted to go back to the fort, but I told them that it was only a spy and that we may as well have all the fun ourselves. By the time we had mounted our horses the Indian had crossed the creek and was gliding through the trees at remarkable speed. I unslung my rifle and began shooting at him, but a running Indian is not an easy mark and I missed every shot. The Indian ran for a bluff some four hundred yards distant. We knew that we could not ride our horses over such a barrier and if we tried to go down to the nearest place that it could be ascended, the Indian would get too good a start, so we quit our horses and followed afoot.

. . .When the Indian saw me begin to leave the other boys he began running faster. The other men stopped and began firing at him, but the trees were so thick they could not get a good aim at him. They shouted to me to stop, that the Indian would lead me into some trap. I was too excited to heed what they said. . .

Doubtless the Indian thought I would soon give out, but when I had kept his pace for about a mile. . .we came to a bend in the creek and the Indian seeing he would save two or three hundred yards by cutting across, made a dash. I dropped upon my knees and took aim, but before I had time to shoot the Indian reached a small oak tree. An arrow came whizzing through the air and I had to dodge. As fast as I could raise my gun the Indian would send an arrow at me with such accuracy that the situation began to look serious to me. I was afraid that he would send one that I would not be able to dodge, and so I raised my rifle and shot. I threw up my arm and his last arrow went through the muscle just below the elbow and stuck in my neck. I then went to the Indian and found he had been hit almost in the center of the forehead. . .

My three comrades soon came up and they buried the Indian under an oak tree in a narrow grave, which we dug with a hatchet and the butts of our guns. We rode back to the fort. On account of my arrow wound, another man was put in my place in the party which was to go back to Fort Worth, and as soon as my term was up I settled on this ranch. . .

I thought then that I had done something great but now since the years have passed and I have had much time for reflection, the killing of that Indian has become one of the regrets of my life. Every time I pass that oak tree in my lower pasture, I feel sad at the thought of the man that I killed under it.

Frank R. Murray, *Southwestern University Magazine*, 1913

TEXAS LOST ★ ★ ★ ★ ★ ★ ★ ★
Wamba, Texas

More than a century ago, folks in this tiny community north of Texarkana decided to name their crossroads position on what now is FM 1397. There was much debate. The name selected—**Wamba**—came from the most popular brand of coffee being sold in the one store.

JUNE 11, 1865
[On this day] The State Treasury of Texas, for the first and only time, was robbed by armed bandits of $17,000.

Texas Day-By-Day, 1979

THE NEWTON, KANSAS, GENERAL MASSACRE

One McCloskey was known throughout Newton as an errant bully, a swashbuckling braggart, and dangerous to boot, who was always looking for trouble and anxious to add to his reputation as a bad man. But one friend in the world did McCloskey have. This was Riley, a gangling, sunken-chested youth, in the last stages of consumption, whose hollow cheeks, burning eyes, and ever-recurring spasms of coughing told their own story.

There was some mysterious bond between the two. . . They made a strangely assorted pair—the fierce, fire-eating gunman, and the pale, inoffensive, sickly youth.

The trouble began on the morning of August 9. McCloskey, full of drink, thought to ruffle it with a band of Texas cowboys which had just come to town. He picked the wrong bunch. The Texans included in their number two brothers, Jim and Richardson Anderson. . . Hot words were spoken. McCloskey and the Texans separated and within ten minutes the whole town knew that the older Texas brother, Jim Anderson, and McCloskey were gunning for each other [but] it was not until evening fell that the meeting took place.

McCloskey, followed by his shadow, Riley, went to the dance house of Perry Tuttle for refreshments. Here the roistering McCloskey took a noisy part in the proceedings, while Riley, weak from coughing, leaned against the wall near the door, and watched him with bright, feverish eyes.

The door was suddenly flung open, framing the frowning face of Jim Anderson, drawn revolver in hand, while behind stood his brother and friends. Only a second did the scene remain thus. McCloskey's hand streaked for his holster, but it got there too late. His shot was a fraction of a second after his rival's and did no harm. But Anderson's bullet was through McCloskey's brain. The Texans strode in and stood looking down at the body of the man who had affronted them.

And now occurs the strangest part of the story. Riley, the inoffensive. . .seemed transformed into a killing beast by the death of his only friend.

Before the Texans could realize what was happening, he had crossed the room in two lightning bounds, slammed the door and locked it. Then, pulling an old sixshooter. . .with face contorted into a dreadful snarl, and death looking out of his gleaming, slitted eyes, he began to kill.

Men long talked of those next few minutes. The Texans, taken by surprise, turned and fought this new attack. Somebody dashed the light out with a chair, and for seconds only the orange streaks of light from the revolver shots slit the room. . .

Nobody ventured near the building a few minutes; then a bartender entered and lit a light.

A veritable shambles greeted his eyes.

On the floor lay seven men, three dead, four apparently dying. One of the dead men was McCloskey. The other six had all fallen before the fire-spitting revolver of Riley.

Almost on top of McCloskey's body lay Jim Anderson, gasping as if each breath would be his last. Three other members of Anderson's band lay here and there on the floor, with the blood dripping from their wounds.

Thus occurred the "General Massacre." The Texans spirited away their wounded and left town. Riley disappeared.

An account in the *Wichita (Kansas) Eagle*, 1930, of one of the West's most famous gun battles; Frederic Remington painted the scene years later; Riley, whoever he may have been, was never heard from again.

SAGA OF THE GUNMAN AND DEMON RUM

What keeps the name of Clay Allison alive among these oldtimers. . .is not so much the large number of his killings, as the boisterous dare-deviltry, the grim diablerie, with which the man seemed possessed even when he was taking some one's life. Allison sober was an exceedingly pleasant and kind man, but Allison drunk was quite a different being—he became a man dangerous to cross. "He was a whale of a fellow," said a contemporary of Allison, "and considerate of his companions; but throw a drink into him, and he was hell turned loose, rearin' for a chance to shoot-in self defense."

In physical appearance, Clay Allison was a striking, not to say magnificent figure. I have searched hard for a photograph of him, but have never been able to acquire one. Thus for details of his appearance, I have to fall back on word-portraits. He was about six feet two inches in height and weighed between 180 and 190 pounds. He is said to have had the blue eye that seems to have been quite the distinguishing characteristic of the killer, although one who knew him well insists that his eyes were black. His face is described as large, with all its features prominent. Usually there was a serious cast to his countenance; some even speak of it as having a "melancholy look." His hair was worn down to the shoulders, and his mustache was long and formidable, after the fashion of the times. For a man of such large physique, he was remarkably active and quick in his movements. . .

Clay Allison was born in Tennessee about 1840 [and] shortly after the Civil War drifted into the West. . .in what then was called Indian Territory [Oklahoma]. In the course of time Allison drifted. . .into Texas. He seems to have worked for awhile as a cowpuncher at some ranch, probably on the headwaters of the Brazos. . .

While Allison was working in the Brazos section and apparently was on the road to becoming in the course of time one of the cattle kings of that section, he became involved in a serious difficulty with a friend and neighbor. Allison himself never told the cause of the difficulty, but the trouble was so grave it was impossible to settle it amicably. The two men therefore agreed to fight it out.

Allison's grim originality showed itself in the details under which the duel was to take place. It was agreed that a grave should be prepared, of the usual length and width, but with the exceptional depth of seven or eight feet. The two men were to strip themselves to the waist and then seat themselves inside the grave at the two ends, each grasping in his right hand a Bowie knife of a stated size.

At a given signal, they were to arise and start fighting. This they were to keep up until one or the other was dead. A final stipulation required the survivor then and there to cover the dead one with the earth removed in digging the grave. The story gives Allison the victory, but it also attributes to him such a high degree of remorse that it was impossible for him to remain in that vicinity. Therefore he sold out his interests and moved to Colfax County in New Mexico.

"Clay Allison," by Maurice G. Fulton,
Southwest Review, Vol XV, Winter 1930

Fried Soda Crackers

2 c. all-purpose flour

1 tsp. baking soda

1/2 tsp. salt

3/4 c. buttermilk or sour milk

1/4 c. shortening

Stir together flour, soda and salt. Cut in 1/4 cup shortening until the mixture resembles coarse crumbs. Make a well in the dry mixture; add buttermilk or sour milk all at once. Stir just until the dough clings together. Knead gently on lightly floured surface 10 to 12 strokes. Melt enough shortening in deep skillet to give a depth of 1 inch. Heat to 375 degrees. To shape each biscuit, cut off about 1 tablespoon of the dough and farm into a ball about 1 inch in diameter; flatten slightly. Carefully place biscuits, a few at a time, in the hot shortening. Fry until golden, turning once, about 2 minutes per side. Drain. Serve hot. Makes about 24 biscuits.

Traditional

REVIVALS WERE A TEXAS FULL-CONTACT SPORT

Late summer, [religious] revivals were held under brush arbors built in the country. In wagons, buggies, oxcarts, on horseback and on foot, everyone physically able made his way to the arbor for the meeting. Many families brought tents, oftentimes made of the hides of various animals, bedding, and extra clothing.

A crude platform, with seats for the choir and a pulpit for the preacher, was made of split logs placed at one end of the arbor. The seats of the congregation were backless. Many opposed the use of instrumental music in church ritual, so the "singing" was usually led without any accompaniment. The men and boys sat on one side of the arbor during the services and the women and girls on the other. Small children were placed on "pallets" at their mother's feet, with a chicken bone, a crust of bread, or a cookie to gnaw upon. Illumination was furnished by crude kerosene flares, and these usually attracted a variety of insects to annoy the devout listeners.

On certain days, generally Sundays, there was "meeting all day and dinner on the ground." In preparation for these occasions, our mothers spent many hours in their homes cooking many varieties of food. Frequently large rawhide trunks were packed to overflowing to supplement the already filled dinner baskets of truly noble proportions. Great rivalry and pride were evinced by the women in the quality and quantity of food prepared.

After the morning sermon of an hour and a half to two hours, we would form in animated groups under the trees and wait for the older women to call us to dinner, which was spread on snowy homespun table cloths, placed end to end for yards. The minister or some elderly man would say grace, and the consumption of food was begun. . .

The men and women invariably whiled away the hot afternoon hours in conversation. The young folks would go for walks in the "burying ground" and pursue their "sparking" in the way usual everywhere. Small children who could be persuaded to become quiet were put to sleep on quilts under the shade.

Later in the afternoon separate prayer meetings were held for men and women in nearby groves of trees, led by some outstanding man or woman of well known religious habits.

Preaching was fervid and declamatory and was listened to raptly, with the accompaniment of many devout "amens" resounding from the amen corner by the deacons or elders. Frequently, several men and women would shout in the excess of their joyous religious emotion and tenderly embrace friends and relatives. At times, some of the notedly religious men and women would circulate quietly among the congregation and urge the humble objects of their solicitude to turn from the evil of their ways or come up to the "mourner's bench," the front seat where sins were confessed.

Ken Cary, *Bois d'Arc to Barb'd Wire*, 1936

★ ★

FLOSSIE

Name of the little wood-burning steam engine pulling the entire San Antonio, Rio Grande Valley Railroad in 1903 between Edinburg and San Juan; the complete train was Flossie and one car, which ran on eight miles of track.

69

OUTHOUSES STOLEN BY OUTRAGED MOBS

At one house where everything was extremely neat, and where we had silver cups for drinking, there was no other watercloset than the back of a bush or the broad prairie an indication of the queerly Texan incompleteness in cultivation of manners.

From something a German gentleman afterwards told us, it would appear that waterclosets are of recent introduction in Texas. He had lived some time in. . .quite a large settlement, before he had time to erect one of those little social necessaries. Though the first to do so, he had no idea that it was a matter of interest to any other person than himself; but no sooner did it appear, than he was assailed for indecency, and before he well knew on what account, his edifice was torn down and dragged away by a nocturnal mob. He shortly rebuilt it. It again disappeared on the sly. Nothing daunted, he caused a third to be put up, and as the thing was founded on a real want in human nature, it took, and two or three others appeared.

Frederick Law Olmsted, A Journey Through Texas, 1857

★ ★ ★ ★ ★ ★ ★ ★ ★ ★ ★ ★ ★ ★ ★ ★

TEXAS IS HOMEOPATHIC

I am going down the Western slope of life, cannot carry the weights, run the races, nor pack the loads I once could. [But] With Texas air, Texas exercise and Texas habits generally—active, outdoor and bracing—I can go on for years barring accidents and ordinary ills.

Sheep rancher George Wilkins Kendall, in a letter to a friend, January 1867

EARLY TEXANS WERE A LITTLE ROUGH AROUND THE EDGES

At this moment up came dashing across the plain a regular old Kentuck who had been in Texas seventeen years. Said he, "Strangers! where mout you be from?" We told him. Says he, "Maybe ye havn't seen a hoss critter like the one I'm on?"

"No."

"Rot him," says he; "He's a heap of trouble to a feller, though I don't blame him, for them'ar geese and deer eat and pison up right smart of the grass."

"Why don't you shoot and eat them?" said I.

"'Cause they ain' no account, no how."

"Don't your men hunt them at all?"

"No," said he.

"Why, what do you live on?"

"Hog and homony," said he, "and dog; anything else, barring coffee, and I will have a smart chance of that, if I have to run to my neighbor's fort." I asked him how near he had any neighbors. "Oh plenty," said he, "right near. One ten miles and one thirteen miles."

He was barefooted and had on a shirt that might have been worn without washing six months, and like its possessor looked dirty and hideous—disgustingly so. Such is living or staying in Texas with many of the settlers, who are well off, but have no ambition above the brute.

Attributed to "H," in Littell's Living Age, April/June 1847

Τhis Texas of ours is an astonishingly prolific country.... "[B]ut in horned frogs, scorpions, tarantulas and centipedes, we beat the universe. Everybody has seen horned frogs. You see them in jars in the windows of apothecaries. You are entreated to purchase them by loafing boys on the levee at New Orleans. They have been neatly soldered up in soda boxes and mailed by young gentle-men in Texas to fair ones in the old states. The fair ones who receive the neat package from the post office are delighted with the prospect of a daguerreotype—perhaps jewel-ry—open the package eagerly, and faint as the frog in excellent health hops out, upon them. A horned frog is, simply, a very harm-less frog with very portentous horns; it has horns because everything in its region, trees, shrubs, grass even—has horns and nature makes it in keeping with all around it. A menagerie would not be expensive. They are content to live on air and can live, I am told, for several months without even that.

The scorpions are precisely like those of Arabia, in the shape of a lobster exactly, only not more than some three inches long. You are very apt to put one upon your face in the towel which you apply thereto after washing. If you do, you will find the sting about equal to that of a wasp, nothing worse. They are far less poisonous than the scorpion of the East. In fact none, except newcomers, dread them at all.

But the Tarantula!. . .[F]ilthy, loathsome, abominable and poisonous, crush it to atoms before you leave it. If you have never seen it, know henceforth that it is an enormous spider, concentrating in itself all the venom and spite and ugliness of all spiders living. Its body is some two inches long, black and bloated. It enjoys the posses-sion of eight, long, strong legs, a red mouth, and an abundance of stiff brown hair all over itself. When standing it covers an area of a saucer. Attack it with a stick and it rears on its hind legs, gnashes at the stick, and fights like a fiend. It even jumps forward a foot or two in its rage, and if it bites into a vein, the bite is death!

Anonymous, *Arthur's Home Gazette*, February 1853

A CREATIVE LYNCHING

Last night about thirty men rode up to the Mat Wallace's house about three-fourths of a mile from the public square [in Waco], called him out, took him about fifty yards and hung him to a tree. The tree being low they tied a rope to his feet and tied it to another tree to prevent him from touching the ground.

Galveston News, July 23, 1875

★ ★ ★ ★ ★ ★ ★ ★ ★ ★ ★ ★ ★ ★ ★ ★

Kiss Me Quick & Go

Name of featured 1860 cocktail in Bank of Bacchus, a Houston saloon owned by Dick Dowling, later to become the hero of Sabine Pass during the Civil War

THE SIDESADDLE SAGA OF BLUE JOHN AND PONY

He was a buckskin with black points. He was medium size, beautifully formed and very graceful. He was so gentle he seemed a deadhead when wandering about the ranch. Who had trained him, I don't know. My brother bought him when the animal was three years old. He could singlefoot, pace or trot.

His one great passion was running cattle. Every cattleman near him knew him to be the best horse in that section. When on a round-up and each man was separating his cattle from the others, Pony would work tirelessly whirling, turning and tossing his head at everyone disposed of.

My sisters and I rode him everywhere. But later on, he developed a quality, arising from his being high strung, that made him exceedingly hard headed. At times, becoming excited, he would take the bit in his teeth and do as he pleased unless he was ridden by a man and sometimes then he would give the fellow quite a ride before he could pull the horse down.

The country was all open then. There were no pasture fences. My father's ranch at this time was fifteen miles north of Barksdale in Edwards County, on Cedar Creek. It was the roughest country imaginable. There were thick groves of cedar trees every few hundred yards. A winding road ran through the creek around immense boulders and then cedars with now and then, a tiny, grassy plot and then more cedars.

Into this section had wandered a large, blue steer. He belonged to some ranchman further west. He was a longhorn, rather heavy and an utter outlaw when it came to putting him into a corral.

My sisters and I had named him "Blue John." He showed no disposition to fight. On the contrary, he always ran at sight of mankind.

One morning my father, pressed for help, told me to saddle Pony and go to town for some important mail he was expecting. Hurriedly, he warned me to go around all cattle on the first part of the trip—that was, until Pony became too tired to be "peppy."

I started off riding one of those foolish oldtime sidesaddles. It was held in place by a girth and a circingle.

I watched for cattle. Pony kept tossing his head impatiently. Suddenly, it happened. There was Blue John about twenty feet away.

The steer snorted and turned to run. Then began for me a grueling experience. Pony took the bridle bit in his teeth and in high glee, followed Blue John in spite of all I could do. The first leap he made caused the saddle blanket to start slipping. Remember, I was riding a sidesaddle.

Blue John took to the cedar brake. Pony enthusiastically followed. A short time after, the blanket went and thereafter, it required all my wits to keep the saddle from slipping. I knew not what direction we were taking. All my time was taken up in keeping the saddle on the horse's back. In fact, I did not ride the horse, I rode the saddle. Sometimes it was on Pony's withers and sometimes on his hips. I saw nothing and knew nothing but trying to hold that saddle in place. Still, there was no abating of the chase. Down hills, over mountain points, across slippery rocks we went. I was growing exhausted. My long hair became unbraided and whipped around projecting limbs of trees but I jerked it loose, losing many strands.

Down a hill through dangerous limbs of cedars we went. At last, we came to a road. I was too exhausted to recognize it.

And then we reached my father's field fence. Dimly, I seemed to remember it but I was too tired and uncertain of the outcome of this impromptu chase. As we went over the last rise and down it I saw father hurry to open the corral gate. He knew the danger beyond the corral. The country above was too wild for swift riding.

Blue John went into the corral. I had penned him!

Father helped me from the horse and the saddle came off with me.

"I should not have sent you on that horse," he said, regretfully. I didn't answer. My hair was full of cedar sprigs, my dress was torn to shreds. Mother bound up my wounds and fed me.

"Say, young lady," said my father presently, "did you know you penned Blue John?"

"Penned nothing!" I said disgustedly. "It was that horse. He could pen an antelope!"

Dear little Pony.

The Library of Congress, WPA Writers Project; from interview with Letitia Charlton of Edwards County; undated, circa late 1930s

TEXAS VS WOMEN

The women of eastern Texas [in 1857] seemed to us, in general, far superior to their lords. They have, at least, the tender hearts and some of the gentle delicacy that your "true Texan" lacks, whether mistresses of slaves or only of their own frying-pan. They are overworked, however, as soon as married, and care gives them thin faces, sallow complexions, and expressions either sad or sour.

Frederick Law Olmsted, *A Journey Through Texas*, 1869

*I was the first woman. . .*to set foot on the Mott Ranch [Bandera County, 1878], and when the chickens, dogs and stock of all kinds, caught sight of me the shock was too great, and they all took to the brush. The house was just what one might expect it to be— kept by two middle-aged bachelors. Mr. Mott was small, fat, and red, and was very nervous, so much so that when a hen would do her duty by laying an egg, her cackling would annoy him to such an extent that he would rush out and throw stones until she quieted down. Consequently, every fall a wagon load of stones would have to be cleaned out of the corn house before the new crop could be stored. John [Gahagan] was an entirely different type—tall, thin, and gotten up in a most attractive style. He rode a good horse, and always wore a pistol and cartridge belt, high boots, high hat, and red handkerchief around his neck. I think he must have belonged to a better class in Ireland. He was well educated, and spoke of taking fencing lessons which is only taught to people of means. He had beautiful hunting dogs, and was very fond of animals, and on one occasion when he lit the fire to make coffee, he was deeply grieved because he shut the oven door and burnt up his cat.

Mrs. Albert Maverick, San Antonio, remembering life in Texas, about 1878

* * * * * * * * * * * * * * * * * * *

We [in Texas] only had two or three laws, such as against murder before witnesses and being caught stealing horses, and voting the Republican ticket.

O. Henry, *Sixes and Sevens*, 1920

Jerky: Beef or Venison 1850

Take a cut of beef, venison, or other meat except pork. Trim fat from meat. Remove bones. Put meat on a board; sprinkle with salt and pepper and any other spices you desire. Pound in seasoning (or meat may be sliced, then seasoned). Turn over and repeat salting and pounding.

Prepare pan of water for blanching meat—1 qt. water and 1 tbsp. salt. Bring to simmer and hold at that temperature while blanching. Cut meat with grain into strips about 1/2 inch thick or less. Dip each into hot water and hold for 10 to 15 seconds until it turns whitish gray. Hang at once by stringing with looped threads from one end. Prevent contamination from flies, dogs, etc. (Cheesecloth not wrapped tightly may be used.)

Drying rate should be high. Should be done in 3 to 5 days. Jerky will be almost black and will break like a twig. Store in covered jars. May be carried in pockets. Stew may be made by breaking into small bits, searing in a little lard or shortening, and adding a little flour, water, and vegetables.

Delma Cothran Thames,
*A Pinch of This and a Handful of That:
Historical Recipes of Texas*, 1988

Cough. . .

There is no state of greater healthfulness than Texas, while many portions of the state, as Austin and San Antonio and the hilly regions farther north and west, are the resort of consumptives who almost invariably recover and live many years. It is a fact not to be gain-said or denied, that for pulmonary complaints there is no climate in the world more favorable than that of the section we have indicated.

Texas Almanac, 1873

Don't Cough

Consumptives Unwelcome in Texas. . .the people of the state are no longer able to cope with the tuberculosis situation. So many consumptives have been sent to Texas that the death rate from that disease has risen from almost nothing to over 10 per cent, and that the natives are now suffering from the disease because the population is unable to assimilate the added consumptives. The local charitable associations are said to be impoverished and are unable to look after those now in Texas. . . Almost all Texas hotels and private boarding houses refuse to accommodate consumptives.

Dr. W.M. Brumby, "Consumptives Unwelcome in Texas,"
Journal of the American Medical Association, April 3, 1909

A SURE-FIRE CURE FOR THE COMMON COLD

Cures for many. . .diseases were. . .based on folklore, and error, and old wives' tales. Some physicians drew off a cup of blood at the first complaint of a patient, even before the ailment was diagnosed. Brown sugar was believed to be just the thing for smallpox. A Texas rancher posted a prescription for bad colds in his bunkhouse:

ONE QUART OF WHISKEY AND A DOZEN LEMONS.

DIRECTIONS: THROW THE LEMONS AT A FENCE POST AND DRINK THE WHISKEY.

Ross Phares, *Texas Tradition*, 1954

A UNILATERAL CHRISTMAS IN TEXAS' BIG BEND

Elmo and Ada Johnson decided, in 1929, to have an American Christmas for all the Mexican families in the area. Dinner was to be served and gifts given, and Santa Claus was scheduled to appear. The Mexicans knew nothing about our Christmas traditions, and the preparations were on a grand scale. Maria and Andrea Holguin, who had worked in American homes and shared in such Christmas festivities before, did lots of sewing to make Santa's suit and fifty large stockings. Mrs. Johnson began the project in July, as she had to order most of the supplies by mail.

The Johnsons had a Delco power unit, so colored globes and all sorts of illuminated decorations were ordered. Two days before Christmas Eve, I drove to Alpine to pick up last minute items, and on the way back I chopped down an eight foot cedar tree, which we all decorated. Lee Rackley, a young fellow from Boerne, Texas, was recruited to be Santa Claus, and he was eager to don the white wig and beard and the red suit, padded with a pillow.

It was time to send out the "invitations." Alejandro Garcia, who worked for the Johnsons, was to send an *aviso* [verbal message] to every Mexican family within twelve miles of the border. All were invited, but the *aviso* was to stress that children especially were to come, as Santa Claus wanted to meet every boy and girl. Dinner would begin at noon, followed by gift giving at two o'clock.

Most of the words of the message, such as navidad for "Christmas," or *regalos* for "gifts," were easily converted into Spanish, though "Santa Claus," was difficult, for the closest Spanish word is *clausa* ("clause"). I described Santa Claus to Alejandro as being rather like one of the three wise men who visited the infant Jesus.

Shortly before two on Christmas Eve, the large patio of the Johnson home was packed with children and their parents. I was near two boys, both about ten years old, when Santa made his entrance. One exclaimed, "Santo Claus walks just like Lee!" The *aviso* had been understood.

That the shrewd children detected the speaking and walking characteristics of Lee Rackley is nothing more than testimony of the attention those people gave to an individual's mannerisms. The important fact is that the *aviso* communicated all the specifics save for that of displacing the "a" in "Santa" of the Johnsons' gracious invitation.

Ada Johnson must have seen more people happy that Christmas Eve than any other person in the Rio Grande area. Months after the celebration I was in Cuatrocienegas, 180 miles from the Johnson ranch, and several people, upon finding out where I was from, said that they had heard of the Johnsons' *feliz navidad*.

There was a bit of spillover from Alejandro's *aviso*, for, several days after the party, some Mexicans would come to the Johnson ranch asking about gifts and "Santo Claus."

W.D. Smithers, *Chronicles of the Big Bend*, 1976

COWBOYS WERE TOUGH

I am now to tell you of two incidents to illustrate a Texas cowboy's great fortitude under the severest trials, sufferings, and danger. [In the fall of 1880] a chuck wagon hauled in a cowboy with his leg broken. His horse had fallen with him three or four miles east of the cattle trail and broken his leg. The old boy had crawled that three or four miles with that broken leg to the trail, which took him several hours, and this chuck wagon, passing by about 11 p.m. picked him up. I never heard that boy whimper one time. In the year 1885 I was in swimming with a bunch of cowboys, and seeing one with an old knot on his leg, I asked him the cause. He said, "I am the man who crawled the four miles with a broken leg in 1880."

In the year 1884 there were some cowboys roping cattle on the prairie. Two men roped and threw a big bull. One fine, big, stout man, about twenty-five years old, was sitting on the bull's back when the catch rope on the bull's neck broke; of course, as all cowboys know, that slackened the rope around the bull's hind feet, and immediately he leaped to his feet with the cowboy on his back. The bull tossed him up in the air, and he came down on the bull's horns, and the bull ripped him open from his groin to his navel, not however, tearing open his intestines. The men fixed him up as best they could. . . In a few days I went to see him. He was on his back with his legs tied up and out. He was pale but had on his face a courageous smile. I said, "John, have you suffered much?" He said, "No, it's all in the game." The man who had been with him all the time said he never had even grunted. . .

There was in our camp. . .a cowboy who went by the name of Bednego; we never knew what his real name was. This boy was taken sick with pneumonia, and we had him hauled to a doctor about fifty miles from our camp. . . .The doctor said, "Your man is dying and won't live until morning. You had better find out where his people are and ask him if he wants to send any word or message to them." I dreaded the job of telling this old boy but had to do it. . . The boy was propped up with pillows and looked to me to be dying. About all he could take was buttermilk, and he always loved that drink. I said, "Bednego, you know we are your friends, and will stay with you till the last, but you are a very sick man and may not get well. We will do all we can for you; but we want to know, should you not get well, is there any word you want to send to your folks." It seemed to hurt his feelings to think we were weakening when he had no idea of giving up the fight. In a weak voice, between breaths, he said, "Harry, I reckon you better. . .better. . .give me another. . .glass of. . .buttermilk." I said, "Old boy, your kind don't die." We held his head up, and that old puncher sucked slowly at that glass of milk until it was all gone. By morning he was on his way to recovery. . .

H.H. Halsell, *Cowboys and Cattleland*, 1937

How to Fence in West Texas

There is an art to going through [a barbwire] fence and most West Texans learn it from childhood.

Most fences have four strands, rising about four feet high with the bottom strand about one foot from the ground. There is an etiquette of procedure used by two people going through a fence. One of them takes the next-to-top wire in his hand and pulls up while pushing down with his foot on the next-to-bottom strand. Once through, the first person does the same thing from the other side of the fence for the second passer. It is tricky. It requires a certain amount of experience, instinct, and the habit of years to lay the torso parallel to the deadly wires and slip the torso through without slicing coat, shirt, and skin in the movement. The modern two-spike barbs are machinecut and slice like a razor. Older three and four-pronged barbs are simply impossible to traverse.

Getting a woman through a barbwire fence is not so much a process as a performance. Each time it is done it turns out differently, successful or not. Needless to say, in the old days of long, full skirts and multitudes of petticoats, it was tried only in dire emergencies. Barbwire (or "bobwire" as West Texans always say it) seems to have a menacing if inanimate second sense for when a human passing through is nervous or uncertain. It almost cannot be fooled, and even the saggiest, oldest, mildest-appearing fence—even a rickety three-strand relic—will react savagely when approached by a woman. Of course, in contemporary female clothing, the going through a barbwire fence by a woman does offer certain visual prospects which seemingly shy, range-recluse cowboys have been known to take advantage of, for there is no more awkward or revealing posture for even the prettiest, most modest girl than the half-crouch, half-waddle employed, from sheer necessity, in manipulating through two not too widely separated strands of barbwire—while wearing a tight skirt.

It is interesting, although not too historically important, to note that West Texas ranch women were among the last in the country to take up the wearing of men's pants.

A.C. Greene, *A Personal Country*, 1969

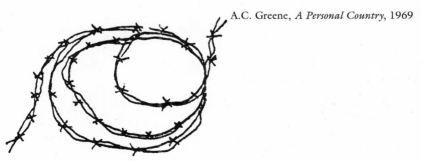

I arrived in Jacksborough on the second day of September, 1869. . . .finding a little frontier town of about five hundred people. On the main street, running back from Lost Creek, there were eight saloons, three stores, and a blacksmith shop, not a bad showing at that, especially when we considered that all the saloons were full fledged gambling houses and five of the number dance halls. Eight-tenths of the population of Jacksborough were gamblers and many of the women were of the lowest class of the underworld. It is no wonder that the only law of the place was backed up by the pistol or rifle. You can readily see that Jacksborough was far from being a paradise, but all the same some of the best, truest, and kindest men and women that ever lived made their place of abode Jacksborough in the late 'sixties and early 'seventies, men who would gladly give their life for a friend, and women who would find no night too dark or storm too hard to go to help any one in need. No man went hungry; no woman unprotected; the rifle and the pistol spoke the law from which there was no appeal. And looking back with the eyes of old age, and with judgment that is matured, I can recall but few mistakes made in their decisions. The man that was killed, it was generally proved, met his just fate. If two men agreed to shoot it out, together they walked out, got ready and began shooting. They were all good shots, and the one that could make the first draw was usually the one that was able to tell the story; the other we would bury. We practiced to be quick and accurate, for no one knew the hour that his life might depend on the first shot and that a sure one.

No man asked another where he came from, why he came, or what he intended to do. They met as equals and parted as friends. Every man's word or credit was good. If he lent a dollar he would receive one hundred cents in payment. I do not remember of a merchant ever losing a bill unless the one owing it died, and then he usually left enough money to pay his debts. That is the way I found West Texas in 1869.

WS. Barlett, *My Foot's in the Stirrup*, 1937

NAMES TO CURL YOUR TEXAS HAIR

Kurls A-Top Beauty Shop.

Make Um' Pretty Beauty Salon

Bob In Beauty Shop

Midget Beauty Shop

Bronco Bowl Salon of Beauty

Cutie Curl Beauty Shop

Skeeterette Beauty Bar

Chat Shak Beauty Salon

Rav On Beauty Salon

Gypsy Hair-A-Van

The House of a Different Do

Monograph: Balma C. Taylor,
Names for Texas Beauty Shops,
Texas A&M University at Commerce, 1974

FIGHTING INDIANS (AND SURVIVING) IN 1855

In the year 1855, Fort Inge was abandoned by the United States troops and business dwindled to dullness itself. Messrs. Black & Stratton laid off the land into lots where Uvalde now stands and commenced selling the lots to the highest bidders. A man named Westfall lived thirty-five miles below on the Leon [River], his only companions being a Frenchman named Louie, his dog "Ketchum," and his gun "Fetchum."

In July, 1855, Indians surrounded his house unseen by any of the inmates of this solitary ranch. Louie was getting dinner, "Ketchum" was taking his morning nap on the floor in the house. Westfall went to the door, not knowing of the danger lurking so near at hand. Just as he reached the door an Indian shot him, the ball taking effect in the upper part of his body. The faithful dog, true to his name and master, sprang out and caught the Indian and brought him to the ground. During the struggle the dog received two shots, causing him to let go his hold and flee into the house where he fell dead. Westfall, feeling so enraged and believing he had received a mortal wound, snatched up his gun and started out to fight them as long as life should last, but Louie implored him to remain in the house, proposing to take a hand himself, and taking deliberate aim he fired at an Indian, then opened the door to ascertain if possible the effect of his shot when a rifle ball passed through the poor fellow's body. He sat down, pulled off his boots and fell dead.

Westfall took position at a crack in the wall to fire at the Indians but they soon left the premises. He was now entirely alone, thirty-five miles from the nearest settlement, and choking with his own life's blood. In this critical condition, he lay four days, envying the Frenchman and the dog, who lay dead a short distance from him. At the end of this time the stench from his former companions became unendurable, and he was compelled to leave the house.

He filled his canteen with water and started to Uvalde. Four days later he arrived at Henry Livering's, where he remained and was in a few weeks well again.

W. W. Arnett, quoted in *The Frontier Times*, July 1923

✦ ✦ ✦ ✦ ✦ ✦ ✦ ✦ ✦ ✦ ✦ ✦ ✦ ✦ ✦ ✦ ✦ ✦ ✦ ✦

Soon after the fall of the Alamo, about April 1836, this announcement was plastered on walls all over New Orleans

THE TEXAS RANGERS: AN ARRESTING INCIDENT

In 1876, as an incident of the Taylor-Sutton feud, Dr. Philip Brazell and son George were called out of their home in Clinton, DeWitt County, by a number of masked riders and killed. Shortly before Christmas Lieutenant Lee Hall of the Rangers was sent into the county with warrants for the arrest of seven men charged with the murder. . .

On the night of December 20, Hall discovered that. . .the men he was looking for were attending the wedding of Joe Sitterlie at the home of the bride's father, near Cuero. He set out with his troop in a driving rain, got to the scene and surrounded the house. Then, unarmed, he went to the front door of the house and announced himself.

The music stopped. Frightened women ran off the dance floor as Bill Meador and other men moved forward.

"What do you want?" Meador asked.

"I have warrants for seven men," Hall answered. And he read the names.

"How strong are you?" demanded Meador.

"Seventeen, including myself," said the lieutenant, following the tradition of telling the exact truth.

"Meador snorted. "We've got seventy!" he announced.

"That's about the right odds," the Ranger said. "We'll fight."

"Listen, all of you," he called out. "You people in the house have three minutes to move out your women and children, starting now. . ." You Rangers," he shouted at the men he had posted in a circle about the house, "at the end of three minutes, fire at will. Now you gentlemen in the house, get the women away. . ."

"I don't want to go killing," Meador answered in a shocked voice. "I'll surrender." And the rest of the wedding guests quickly joined him in handing over their weapons.

Hall collected his prisoners in the gallery at the end of the house and the Rangers were bringing up horses when the bride suddenly ran up to him.

"You're breaking up my wedding party," she accused him brokenly. "Why can't you wait for morning with your old law business."

"Now that you mention it, no reason at all," Hall assured. "Go ahead with your dance."

He sent the prisoners back into the house, reassigned the Rangers so that, turn and turn about, half of them could mount guard while the other half danced, and then joined the party himself. When day broke, he bade goodby to his hostess and rode away to put the chiefs of the Sutton faction in the county jail. There were no hard feelings between the captors and the captives. Meador and his men would have had no compunction about killing the Rangers if the job could have been done gracefully and safely. If compelled, Hall and his troop would have killed the assassins of Dr. Brazell with no qualms whatever. But until necessity arose for the departure from good social usage, there was no reason why they shouldn't all act like gentlemen.

Robert J. Casey, *The Texas Border*, 1950

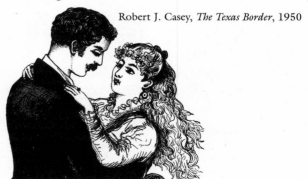

EVOLUTION OF A LEGEND

The cowboy, or "cow boy," as the term was written before he began riding on Hollywood's purple celluloid landscapes, was a kind of Cossack in service to the prairie czars then inventing the American cattle industry. His forefathers were the Spanish conquistadores, his cousins the mountain-men who first ventured into the West, and he was, says historian Paul Horgan, ". . .the last of the clearly traditional characters [born] from the kind of land he worked in and the kind of work he did."

He neither built nor explored nor populated the West but moved ever so briefly across it, as capricious and lonely as the blowing dust. Dime novelists and penny dreadful authors scribbled magniloquent lies about the cowboy for rapt eastern readers but saw him only in town, often ending long cattle drives with a few desperate hours of extravagant carousel before returning to a life of social desolation. Like a cloistered monk of some distant forgotten monastery, the cowboy served his god, the rancher, and toiled at labors decidedly unglamorous. Moving from ranch to ranch, the cowboy made few lasting friendships. He was untutored and ignorant. For endless months he lived on the range, burned in summer, frozen in winter, as punished as the cattle he attended. He slept on the ground under "henskin" blankets. He arose at 4 a.m., or earlier, and often was not asleep again until midnight. He was fed a constant diet of beans ("Pecos strawberries"), greasy stews and Arbuckle's coffee. His aches and sprains were treated with heavy coats of axle grease or prickly pear poultices. To stay awake during long nights of riding herd, he rubbed tobacco juice in his eyes. He lived in a society of men and made love to the only available women, the ubiquitous "Soiled Doves" and "Fallen Angels" on almost a seasonal basis, like some animal in heat. He smelled of the horse he rode, of the cows he tended, and the dung of both.

Miasmic as a nocturne, the cowboy was a neutered man, often profane, never profound, illiterate, itinerant, a harsh child who went crooked or stayed straight or alternated, like an electric current. He hid his past behind such curious aliases as "Shanks" and "Pieface," "Muley," "Stormy," and "Joggy." He observed no religion but the trinity of cow, horse and land. For his always brief entry into towns, he exploded with drunkenness and venery, exchanging six months' wages for a few hours of release from his Trappist confinement. His was a "soulless, aimless" existence, wrote one of the few introspective cowboys who left the range world when he saw it for what it was.

No American character has endured as the cowboy. . . The cowboy lasted little longer than the West, as few as twelve, perhaps as many as a score of years. Behind him came the men with hoes and plows and wives. The cowboy scorned the new arrivals but the farmer lasted; the cowboy did not. He went away to other jobs, went away to other truths, and finally, he just went away.

Jerry Flemmons, *Amon*, 1978

TEXAS POETICAL

Reverie of A Plainsman

Bring back the wagon wheel
    that squeaks,
With a rhythmic cadence that
    even speaks
Of buggy roads where horses trod,
The one with shoes, the other
    unshod;
The faint foot prints of the pert
    horned toad,
The zigzag course of the road
    runner's trail,
The buzzing noise of a rattler's
    tail,
The soaring hawk as the rabbit
    runs
Through parched dry grass from a
    hundred suns. . .
Bring back these things from a day
    gone by.
I'll not complain though the price
    be high,
For on this earth where men reside,
I was born on the prairie side.

Edgar Holmes Neal, 1943

*"You will be traveling
through Indian country and
the safety of your person
cannot be vouchsafed
by anyone but God"*

Disclaimer for passengers heading into West Texas
by the Butterfield Overland Stage Company, 1861, quoted in
That Old Overland Stagecoaching, by Eva Jolene Boyd, 1993

It was quite a fad among West Texas news-paper men during the '80s to combine vers-es, rhymes, and jingles with advertising. The length of the verses depended upon the price the advertiser was willing to pay. The follow-ing lines from the *Mason News,* January 5, 1889, are typical:

The ladies of Mason, bless their
    sweet lives,
The radiant maidens and the
    good queenly wives
Dress finer than any who dwell
    in the West
Because Smith and Geistweidt
    sell them the best.

William Holden,
Alkali Trails, 1930

A TACKY LETTER TO SAM HOUSTON

Webbers Purray 7 January 1842

Sir Old Sam:

We did heare that you was goin to move the seat of government and the publick papers and that you swore you would do it, and then when you come to Austin and found out the boys would not let you do it you said you never was goin to move it. Now Sam you told a dam lie for you did promise the people in Houston that you would move it and I heard a man say that you told Hockley not to bring all his servants because you would all go back soon. But the truth is that you are afeard you Damn old drunk cherokee. We don't thank you because we would shot you and ever dam waggoner that you could start with the papers. You cant do it and we ax you no odds. Travis and Bastrop Fayette Gonzales can bring 1,000 men out and Ned Burleson and Lewis P. Cook have promised that you shant budge with the papers. I heard them myself and you know Burleson and Cook can make you squat you dam blackguard Indian drunk. Now old fellow if you want to try Ned Burleson's spunk just try to move these papers and old Ned will serve you just as he did your cherokee brother when you took the hat whot you give it to your Daddy Bowler. You shall hear more from me when I am ready.

John Welsh

President Sam Houston wanted to move the Republic of Texas capital from Austin to Houston. Austinites, of whom John Welsh was typical, were against the idea.

★ ★

WASHIN' AWAY OL' SAM'S SINS

Sam Houston shocked the state with his immersion in the "Baptizing Hole" in Rocky Creek, near Independence. Ever since their marriage [his wife] Margaret had been waging a quiet campaign for his soul; Houston's behavior had undergone astonishing improvement, but piety still escaped him. When a friend later teased him about his sins being washed away, Houston, recalling his drinking and swearing and days with the Cherokees, replied, "I hope so, but if they were all washed away, the Lord help the fish below."

James Haley, quoted in *Texas: An Album of History*, 1985

TEXAS EATS

Two Ways to Cook Rattlesnake

Roasted

Skin rattlesnake and cut into pieces. Place pieces on a skewer and put the skewer over glowing coals and keep it turning. When the meat quits sizzling it is done. For a different treat, roll the cooked meat in a flour tortilla with refried beans and eat it like a sandwich.

Trail Boss's Cowboy Cookbook, 1988

Fried

A 3-to-4-footer is the best eating size. Cut off the head, let the body drain, and skin from head to tail. Rattlesnakes are fun to skin. The skin strips off easily except for the point at which the tail bulges slightly just in front of the rattles. A few slices with a knife will finish the job. Slit the belly up the middle. The entrails are easy to remove, leaving almost all meat. Cut the body cross-wise in 1-to-2-inch lengths. The chunks are then rolled in beer batter and fried. Or if you prefer, the meat can be rolled in cornbread before frying. In either case, lightly salt and pepper the meat before coating with batter of meal. Allow 1/3 pound of meat per serving.

Mike Hughes,
The Broken Arrow Ranch Cookbook, 1985

FIRST NIGHT IN TEXAS

I again [1827] took up the line of march for Texas, this time on board a coasting schooner owned by parties in New Orleans, chartered by Carlysle & Smith and laden with supplies for the Mexican army. A steam tug towed us out to the mouth of the Mississppi as far as steamers ventured. The weather was lovely as a dream of Venice, and we founded the Balize[?] and sped away on the wings of the tradewinds over the placid waters. We passed Galveston Island in plain view. There was no sign of human habitation on it, nothing to give promise of the thriving city which now covers it. It was only noted then as having been the rendezvous of Lafitte and his pirates and as such was pointed out to me. The trip was a delightful one and I was in fine spirits, when on the third day we threaded the Paso Caballo and ran into Matagorda Bay, having made the run in a little over forty-eight hours, a remarkable record in those days. We cast anchor in the mouth of the Lavaca River, where we had calculated to find the Mexican troops, but the movements of the troops, as well as the government, were very uncertain, and there were no troops, no agent, no one authorized to receive the goods. There was not an American there. The colonization law exempted from settlement all land within twenty-five miles of the coast; so the territory was given over to the Karankawa Indians, a fierce tribe, whose hand was against every man. They lived mostly on fish and alligators with a man for fete days when they could catch one. They were the most savage looking human beings I ever saw. Many of the bucks were six feet in height, with bows and arrows in proportion. Their ugly faces were rendered hideous by the alligator grease and dirt with which they were besmeared from head to foot as a defense against mosquitoes. . .

It was a dreary place for a lone stranger to land. A few Mexicans came around, but they spoke no English, and I understood no Spanish. At length two men, Fulcher and McHenry, who had squatted on land six or eight miles up the river, sighted the schooner and came down in a dugout. They took me in with them and I spent my first night in Texas in their cabin. My first meal on Texas soil was dried venison sopped in honey. After having spent some months in New Orleans, where everything of the known world was obtainable, it looked like rank starvation to me. . .

Noah Smithwick, *The Evolution of a State, or Recollections of Old Texas Days*, 1900

★ ★ ★ ★ ★ ★ ★ ★ ★ ★ ★ ★ ★ ★ ★ ★ ★

AN ENGLISHMAN FIGURES TEXAS OUT

I shall know pretty well about all south-western Texas by the time we finish this trip. All the cattle-men one comes across are the very essence of good-humour and open-handedness; the great failing with them is that they can't keep out of the bar-rooms, and this is the reason why one hears such an account of the dangers about here. If they went about their business in a sober way, and didn't get into rows in gambling-halls and bar-rooms, they wouldn't be always getting killed.

William Hughes, in an 1878 letter home to England, quoted by Thomas Hughes, *G.T.T. Gone to Texas*, 1884

PIGEON PRESS

Not until I had made several trips [about 1915] from San Antonio to the Big Bend was I trusted by the local people. The credibility I finally achieved was threatened when I started filing stories with the *San Antonio Light*, 350 miles away, by carrier pigeon. The people of the Big Bend thought I was sending intelligence about smuggling to the authorities. I finally was "cleared" when Wayne Cartledge, owner of the Castolon Trading Post, read aloud my news story in Spanish before releasing the bird. One pigeon, shortly before this episode, had set a record for carrying the longest story—a full 8 1/2 x 11 inch page—although he took 10 hours and 15 minutes to get to San Antonio, by no means a speed record.

W.D. Smithers, *Chronicles of the Big Bend*, 1976

A TEXAS UNICORN

A Mr. Knight rode into Cleburne a few days ago on a horned horse. The animal was in every respect a well formed two-year-old colt except that it has two horns about 15 inches long growing from the top of its head. The curiosity is to be sold to a northern showman.

Bastrop Advertiser, October 25, 1883

THE HANDY-DANDY GOURD

The gourd was a very handy vegetable that grew on the frontier of Texas. Early settlers used them for various purposes, and to good advantage. When cut in the proper way they served as dippers, water jugs, spoons and dishes. My mother used a large gourd in which to keep sugar, another in which to keep lard, and still another in which to keep her coffee. The long-necked gourd made an ideal dipper. Ask any old timer how he would like to have a gourd full of cold spring water, and he'll tell you it is the most refreshing drink in the world. The early Texas Rangers and Minute Men, while out on their scouts after Indians, carried water gourds, a dumbbell shaped affair, tied to the horn of their saddles. The method of cleaning out these gourds in preparing them for use, was to fill them with water, and put in a lot of sugar, letting them soak overnight, and then the next morning pour the water out. After drying for a few hours the gourd would be placed on a red ant hill, and the ants would soon remove all of the fibrous growth inside for the sugar that remained. It would then be ready for use, the "gourd taste" having entirely disappeared.

J. Marvin Hunter, *Frontier Times*, August 1935

TEXAS LOST ★ ★ ★ ★ ★ ★ ★ ★ ★ ★
Mecca, Texas

Despite its Islamic name, Mecca, in northwest Madison County, was staunch Baptist territory. It flourished in late 1890s, even had a post office until 1908, then slowly faded away.

☀ TEXANESE ☀

Mule Egg

A kind of joke, but one with a little substance. Once upon a time, northern city folks didn't know much about western rural areas. Such as: an industrious Texas Boy Scout could make a small fortune selling horned frogs to other—read "Yankee"—Boy Scouts at the national annual Jamboree. And cuckle burrs were valuable when touted as porcupine eggs. In this rural/urban deceptive trade practice, a watermelon became a "mule egg." Thus, any large deceit acquired the reputation of being a "mule egg."

Two-Tailed Dog

The full phrase was "crazier than a. . ." or "dumber than a. . ." because a dog, being an ever optimistic creature, wags its tail hopefully to show things are fine even when they're not. And if one wagging tail was good, two were better. So, an always-elated, upbeat-in-the-face-of-all-adversity human was characterized as a "two-tailed dog,"—someone who displayed cheerfulness amid chaos, and was considered a little strange.

TEXAS & WOMEN

We wanted to come [in 1869] to a new place so our children could grow up with the country. I came willing (my husband said he could live ten years longer in Texas); and I have never regretted it one moment, but oh, how sorry I was to leave our Mississippi home where six of my children were born; four came with us, two were left back in Shady Grove graveyard.

We finally got to a place in Texas now called Morgan [Bosque County]. It was then the Nichols Place. Then on to Dr. Russell's on Steel's Creek. I remember well what a dinner we had. There was a large dish filled with turnips and the greens cooked together with a large square of beef that looked exactly like streaked bacon. I thought it was the best thing I had ever tasted, so I handed my plate for a second helping.

Dr. Russell killed a wild turkey soon after we got here that weighed twenty pounds dressed. We could hear the turkeys gobble every morning just before day. We bought a beef weighing 800 pounds for seven dollars. We had pork but no dainties. I made all my own soap. I did all my own washing, made all the clothes for the family. Kept them clean. They never went with holes in their clothes or stockings. . .

Women, they stayed at home and did the work. I would work hours at night after I had put my little children to bed. Sometimes I could do more at night than I could in daytime.

Letter written by the mother of John A. Lomax,
quoted in The Adventures of a Ballad Hunter, *1947*

INDIANS WERE MULTICULTURAL

The Texas Indians are. . .a rather homogeneous entity. All are members of the Mongoloid race and belong to its American Indian subdivision. The physical variations of Texas Indians were minor. . . being confined to slight differences in stature and skin color. If the differences in the behavior of various peoples were rooted in their varying race or biology, we should expect all Texas Indians to have had similar, if not identical, customs and patterns of behavior. Nothing could be further from the actual case. The various tribes of Texas Indians were about as diversified in their behavior as Texans, Frenchmen, Chinese, and Bantus are in theirs.

William Wilmon Newcomb, Jr., *The Indians of Texas*, 1961

A STAMPEDE RECALLED

We hadn't much more'n got to the herd when the air freshened an' things was gettin' right. Then it got cold an' we could hear it comin'. Thunder and lightnin' seemed to spring out of the mesquites. The foreman passed the word: 'Hold 'em till they git wet,' an' we began to circle. The cattle was on their feet in a second, with the first cold air; but we got the mill [circling] started by the time the storm hit. I've seen lightnin'. . .but thet was lightnin' right. As far as thet's con-sarn', I've seen balls o' fire on the end of a steer's horn many a time, but there was a ball o' fire on the end of both horns of every one of them thousin' steers, an' the light in the balls of their eyes looked like two thousin' more. Talk about a monkey wrench fallin' from a windmill an' giving you a sight o' the stars, or one of them Andy Jackson fireworks clubs puttin' off Roman candles at a Fort Worth parade! They're just sensations; this here show I'm tellin' you about was a real experience. We seen things.

A composite cowboy's cattle drive memory, as imagined by Frank Hastings, *A Ranchman's Recollections*, 1921

LIFE ON THE CHISHOLM TRAIL

We are holding on the Little Washita [River] and are getting along very well, but I am satisfied that Forsythe's men beat me out of eleven head. He gathered them right where I had a stampede. . . Our horses are very poor and sick. We had ten stolen a week ago. Everybody is down on a Texas herd and are strictly on the steal. If our horses dont die or some rascal dont steal them we can hold the cattle until about the middle of July, but I will ceep [sic] coming up the trail untill I am Stop.

Trail Boss John McCroskey, in a letter home, cited by Chris Emmett in *Shanghai Pierce: A Fair Likeness*, 1953

THREE TEXAS TOWNS WITH THE SAME NAME

1. *Sweetwater* (English; Nolan County)
2. *Agua Dulce* (Spanish; Nueces County)
3. *Mobeetie* (Indian; Wheeler County)

TAKES ONE TO KNOW ONE

Frontier judges were likely to lose patience with lawyers who spent too much time arguing over points of law. During a bitter altercation in a Texas court, one lawyer shouted at the other: "You are a lying son of a bitch!" His opponent immediately shot back: "You are a lying son of a bitch yourself."

At this, the judge banged his gavel for order, then let silence hang over the room full of spectators who were certain he would levy a heavy fine upon the offending lawyers.

Instead, the judge leaned forward, fixing his gaze first on one and then the other of the attorneys, and said slowly: "Now that you gentlemen have got acquainted with each other, we will proceed with the argument."

Marshall Brown, *Wit and Humor of the Bench and Bar*, 1899

★ ★ ★ ★ ★ ★ ★ ★ ★ ★ ★ ★ ★ ★ ★ ★ ★

TEXAS JUSTICE IS BLIND (DRUNK)

The chief justice of the San Antonio district has among his peculiar habits a set rule to be already in an intoxicated trance by 9 o'clock in the morning.

Prince Carl of Solms-Braunfels, describing Texas and Texans in his emigrant's guide, 1846

The Texas Legislature consists of 181 people who meet for 140 days once every two years. This catastrophe has now occurred sixty-three times. The Legislature is, among other things, the finest entertainment in Texas. It beats the zoo any day of the week.

Molly Ivins, *The Atlantic*, March 1975

OUR LEGISLATURE IN EARLY TEXAS (IT'S A JOKE)

The congress extraordinary of the rounders of the republic of Texas, will convene at the grand hall above the Bexar Exchange, on Saturday the 25th. All distinguished rounders of the republic are invited to attend. Several members have already arrived; among them are the members from Screw-Auger Creek, Screamersville, Schubatansville, Squizzlejig County, Toe Nail, Kamchatka, Epidemic, Hyene's Hollow, and Racoon's Ford.

The dictator-general of the rounders of the republic is hourly expected. The message of his excellency is expected to combine originality, vigor, philosophy, and sage advice to the members of the fraternity. We are requested to publish the two subjoined rules, and call the particular attention of members to their provisions prior to the commencement of business:

"If any member is too drunk to rise from his seat to speak, the chair shall appoint a committee of three to hold him up; but provided the member shall be dead drunk, and unable to speak, the chair shall appoint an additional committee of two to speak for him; provided, however, that if the member is able to hold up by tables, chairs, etc., then, and in that case, one of the committee shall gesticulate for him."

Austin Daily Bulletin, 1841

I WAS JUST TURNING MY SIXTH YEAR WHEN I ATE MY FIRST BISCUITS. . .

It's a fact, and I was lucky to get 'em then for flour was not in general use until I was about 20. People all raised little patches of corn and bread made from that was all we had. Father took a trail herd up the year I was 6 and when he delivered it and collected the money he spent some of it for a wagon and flour enough to load it to the full. When he drove home with all that flour it was some sight.

All of the neighbors came to see and share in it; for of course he let them have their part. I'll never forget it if I live to 100, how anxious I was to taste bread made of that white soft flour. Nor how good those first biscuits were. We saved every tiny crumb, for corn bread had never been plentiful enough to waste and biscuits were on a basis with cake those days. . .

I was 16 years old before I had a pair of shoes that I could actually wear all the time. Rawhide was our only shoe material and all you could say for it was the hair was taken off. Talk about hard, dry, stiff, unbendable leather—that rawhide had the world beat and a mile to go on.

If they were big enough to avoid all this trouble you couldn't walk in them, especially hunting, and we just had to hunt, for it was no trick at all to kill a big buck deer or antelope, a buffalo or all the wild turkey we could carry. And it was too much fun to give up just to wear shoes.

A fellow with a grain of sense would rather trust to the calluses on his soles than to risk losing a shot and rubbing blisters on his feet with those rawhide hobbles.

I might say honestly that I never did have any real shoe or boot comfort until I got my first pair of high-heeled, high-topped, hand-made cowboy boots. I still wear that kind, too, and always will for th're as much a part of me and every other open-range cowpuncher as his leather leggings, spurs and broad-brimmed hat.

Cowboy/rancher Jim Rose, quoted in the *Dallas SemiWeekly Farm News*, April 8, 1927

★ ★ ★ ★ ★ ★ ★ ★ ★ ★ ★ ★ ★ ★ ★ ★ ★

"One day, I reviewed my life as a cowboy from every angle and came to the conclusion that all I had gained was experience, and I could not turn that into cash, so I decided I had enough of it, and made up my mind to go home, get married and settle down to farming."

F.M. Polk, Luling, Texas, in a letter written about 1925

How to Make a Stew and Cuss, All at the Same Time

Back in the early days, roundup was serious business to the cowboy. It was held in the springtime when cattle outfits pitched it together to sort out the stock that had gotten mixed up on the winter range. Calves were branded and cut (castrated), cattle were worked, cowboys signed on for the season. A period of long days' work and short nights' rest began.

A good cook could attract good hands, so during roundup they worked to show their stuff. Son-of-a-Bitch was the customary meal served for the occasion, and camp cooks did their best to make a more delectable stew than their neighbors.

The origins of this famous cowboy stew are lost. Some say the stew originated with the Indians, who ate organ meats for both physical and spiritual sustenance. Perhaps the stew came from some Scottish range cook who hated to waste anything. However the stew was invented, it's a good bet that the first diner said, son-of-a-bitch but that's good, and the name stuck. Whenever a line preacher or a woman came to chuck, the name was sometimes softened to son-of-a-gun, but the stew remained the same.

According to Uncle Dick, my grandfather—who was a ranch foreman—carefully chose the first animal to be slaughtered at roundup. For a good Son-of-a-Bitch, a milk-fed calf was best because the marrow gut, which is actually the connecting tube between two stomachs, was filled with partially digested milk solids, the secret flavoring of a good Son-of-a-Bitch. After the calf was killed and bled, the meat was turned over to the cook.

Old Cookie dug a fire trench, built him up a good fire, then let it burn down to a nice even bed of coals. He hung his pots from iron rods. He placed a Dutch oven—half filled with water—over the coals and let it come to a good rolling boil. First he threw in diced pieces of skinned tongue and heart. After these had cooked and tenderized awhile, he added sweetbreads, kidneys, lungs (called "lights"), a little liver, and the essential marrow gut, carved into rings. Sometimes brains, precooked separately with a little flour until they became "beady," were added to the stew. Occasionally an onion—known to the cowboys as a "skunk egg"—was tossed in.

Skunk eggs were the only concession to vegetables. No corn, limas, potatoes, or tomatoes ever found their way into a bona fide Son-of-a-Bitch. Uncle Dick says it was real good to smell this on the first day of roundup. One of the chief signals that spring had come at last.

The stew bubbled slowly all day. Cookie would cuss a blue streak at anyone who raised dust around the chuck wagon, the cowboys would cast an approving eye toward the pot swinging over the glowing coals, and at last, after a hard day's work, the boys would stand around the chuck wagon until Cookie hollered, come and get it, boys. Then each would take his turn dipping out a tin plate full of Son-of-Bitch, grabbing a sourdough biscuit, and hunting for a proper place to "set" while he ate his favorite meal.

Son-of-a-Bitch was always the first meal after a beef was killed. As the summer wore on and the boys moved the herd up the trail, the stew might be less carefully constructed, but on the day when several outfits pitched in together to sort the herds, it was usual for each outfit to claim that his cook made the best damn Son-of-a-Bitch on the high plains.

When I asked Uncle Dick why people don't eat Son-of-a-Bitch anymore, he snorted, arched his eyebrows, flicked the ash off his cigarette with his little finger and said, hell. Nobody can pick 'em. Nobody can dress 'em and nobody can cook 'em.

Linda West Eckhardt, *The Only Texas Cookbook*, 1981

★ ★ ★ ★ ★ ★ ★ ★ ★ ★ ★ ★ ★ ★ ★ ★ ★ ★

AT LAST, TEXANS GET SIX-SHOOTERS

The first sidearms used in Southwest Texas weren't sidearms. They were tremendous affairs eighteen inches long with a bore of about an inch, single shot, unrifled, equipped with a ponderous flint lock. They weren't sidearms, because they were too cumbersome to be worn on the body. They were carried on horseback, one on the near side and one on the off side of the horse. Even at that, although their effective range couldn't have been over a hundred feet, they must have created considerable consternation among the Indians against whom they were used. . .

The first really effective six-shooter used in Texas, that means the whole world, was a Colt. Much has been written about Captain Samuel Colt and a digest of his history and the history of his firearms couldn't be given here. But, the Captain ranged

around Corpus Christi for a considerable length of time. One day as folklore has it, the Captain got a chunk of wood and with his pocket knife whittled out what he thought would be a model for a swell six-shooter. As we look at it today, this old six-shooter, when turned to brass and iron, was a terrible looking affair. However, in the hands of Captain Jack Hays, the grandest Texas Ranger that ever lived, and in the hands of his company of frontiersmen, the six-shooter certainly played hell with the Indians. Our poor benighted red brethren were not accustomed to finding one man with at least twelve shots.

Frost Woodhull, county judge, Bexar County, writing in *Plaza Parade*, October 1935

1. Light as air
2. Stronger than whiskey
3. Cheaper than dirt

Three claims made by John Gates about the newfangled barbed wire he was trying to sell Texas ranchers in 1876.

TEXAS LOST ★ ★ ★ ★ ★ ★ ★ ★
Hide Bug School

A now long-abandoned rural one-room school near Spur in Dickens County. The name, legend says, described an infestation of bugs in the large stacks of buffalo hides stored in adjacent pastures.

When our own land
forsakes us Texas takes us.

Traditional 19th Century couplet

COWBOY ATTACKS FENCE POST

The opposition to the old time drift fence often reached the state of positive action of some kind. In the early days a drift fence was erected in what is now the north part of Schleicher County, and as this fence controlled much land not owned by the fence owners there was considerable dislike to the fence. The "old-timers" would often take it down and leave it down when it obstructed their path. It became common sport for the boys living nearby to meet and practice roping the posts of this fence. With their ponies at a dead run, they would cast their loops and then see how far they could drag the posts and fence.

The crowd once prevailed upon a newcomer—a long, tall, rough lad—to try his hand at it. He was new at the game but was more than anxious to show that he was a jolly good fellow. Accordingly, he chose the largest fence post that he could find so as to better demonstrate his skill. The post he chose was a corner post and had been placed there to stay. The cowboy made a perfect throw. The loop settled nearly over the top of the post and came to rest on the top wire. The onlookers were thrilled. All went well until the slack in the rope was taken up by the running pony and then "business picked up" in a hurry.

The saddle girth snapped and the saddle and the cowboy came to a sudden and unexpected stop. The onlookers doubled up with mirth, but the ungainly cowboy got up with the remark that they could fence up all West Texas if they wanted to, he'd be damned if he cared.

R. D. Holt, *West Texas Historical Association Yearbook,*
Vol. IV, June 1928

THEY JUST DON'T MAKE RATTLESNAKES THE WAY THEY USED TO

A man living in Kimble county killed the largest snake recently that was ever heard of in this country. The snake was found on the head of the South Llano, in Crockett county, and it measured over eleven feet in length, twenty-seven inches in circumference, ten in diameter, and seven inches between the eyes. It had twenty-one rattles and one button. Its fangs were nearly two inches in length and a large knitting needle could easily be run through their tubes, through which the monster shot poison into its victim.

Hamilton Herald, Summer, 1884

TEXAS POPULATION AUGUST 1836

Americans: 30,000
Negroes: 5,000
Mexicans: 3,500
Indians: 14,000

WHY TEXAS IS VERY UNALASKA-LIKE

It happened that Texas had already made the acquaintance and taken the measure of Alaska in a kind of scouting attack. Some of us had pointed out that Alaska was most likely a figment of imaginations at work up there during those long winter nights.

There are only a few minor things wrong with Alaska, and it was inevitable that hospitable Texas folk would tell them how to straighten things out. . . Alaska basically is a state that has spread itself too thin. It would have progressed faster if it had concentrated some place.

People have argued that there is just as much of nothing in the Big Bend of Texas as there is in Alaska. There is a difference, however. In the Big Bend, nothing is squeezed up close together. In Alaska, nothing has been allowed to run wild.

Alaska runs to foolish exaggeration in a lot of things. Bears, for instance. Alaska produces one-ton bears, which is a useless and silly practice. A five-hundred-pound bear is enough.

And Alaska has mountains you can't climb, so what's the point of them?

In a lot of things, however, Alaska and Texas are complementary, and they can help each other out. Alaska, for instance, has spectacular scenery everywhere but no roads to get to it. Texas has virtually all the fine highways in the world, but a lot of them don't seem to be going any place.

Paul Crume, *A Texan at Bay*, 1961

A SOCIAL NOTE
From
The Texas Monument
February 15, 1854

Married — January 11th, by J.R. Hines, esq., Capt. Kratz, aged 83 years to Miss Eliza Horn, all of Washington County.

On the day following, Mrs. K. had born a fine, likely boy. Mrs. K. and the boy are both doing well, and the Captain has a smile for everyone he meets. The boy has been named Jerome Bonaparte Robertson Kratz!

Quoted by Donald Day, *Big Country: Texas*, 1947

★ ★ ★ ★ ★ ★ ★ ★ ★ ★ ★ ★ ★ ★ ★

TEXAS LOST ★ ★ ★ ★ ★ ★ ★ ★
Lee's, Texas

From the beginning, about 1907, the apostrophe was all important because this remote community in far north Glasscock County was Lee's Store, operated by a Dr. Lee, who also rented rooms to, and treated patients in, his adjacent hotel. The patients had tuberculosis and West Texas' dry air was recommended as a cure. Regardless, Lee's became the only Texas settlement with a government-approved apostrophe. It's still there, on FM 33 (south of Elbow), but the hotel and apostrophe have been lost to history.

TEXAS GETS A FLAG

Organized by William Ward in Macon, Georgia, following a town meeting in November 1835, the "Georgia Battalion of Permanent Volunteers" holds a special place in the Texas saga.

Ward enlisted about 120 men. . .and armed, supplied, and transported them to Texas at personal expense and with the aid of the State of Georgia arsenal. The battalion passed through Knoxville, Georgia, where Johanna Troutman—called the "Betsy Ross of Texas"—presented them with her "Flag of the Lone Star." Hand sewn of white silk embroidered with a single blue five-pointed star, the banner bore the mottoes "Liberty or Death" (some accounts have it "Texas and Liberty" and "Ubi Libertas Habitat, Ibi Nostra Patria Est"—"Where Liberty Dwells, There Is Our Country". . .

It was the Troutman flag that [Colonel James W.] Fannin raised over Presidio La Bahia [at Goliad] on March 8, 1836, upon hearing that the Convention had declared Texas independent on March 2. The imagery of the battalion's "Lone Star" flag proved a timeless and compelling emblem among the Texans.

The first Texas Congress adopted this Lone Star flag as the official banner and sent some of Santa Anna's captured silver service to Johanna Troutman in appreciation. She died in Georgia in 1879. In 1913 Texas Governor O.B. Colquitt secured permission to have her remains brought to Texas for internment in the State Cemetery, where a bronze statue was erected as a monument to her memory. Her portrait hangs in the Senate chamber of the Texas state capitol.

Craig H. Roell, *Remember Goliad!* 1994

CORPORATE LAW

Whenever they could do so, Westerners liked to have fun with the mighty railroads, taunting and teasing, obstructing and annoying. During the time that Ben Thompson, a gambler-gunman-lawman, was marshal of Austin, Texas, the railroad refused to cooperate with him in a certain legal matter, and he resolved to square accounts. An elite daily express train was the pride of the road, keeping to exact schedules, the engineers boasting that watches could be set by their arrivals and departures. One day Ben Thompson drove his buggy upon the track right in front of the locomotive just as it was preparing to pull out. At the first emission of steam, Thompson covered the engineer with his revolver and ordered him to hold the train.

In a leisurely manner the marshal then called to acquaintances on the station platform and carried on bantering talk with them for several minutes while the engineer cursed and fumed. When Thompson was certain that the express would be late at its next station, and probably all along the line, he slowly picked up his reins, slapped his horse into motion, and rolled the buggy off the tracks with a parting shout at the engineer: "You needn't think, sir, that any corporations can hurry me!"

Richard Harding Davis,
The West from a Car Window, 1892

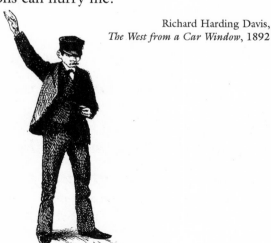

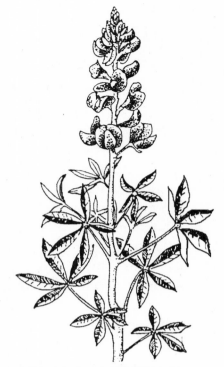

TEXAS' IMMORTAL SPRING

My duties at Jacksboro for the past month [March 1867] had been entirely indoors, and I was not prepared for the beautiful and enchanting appearance of the landscape, as I now for the first time saw the prairies in all their spring beauty. The gorgeous wild flowers, covering the green sward in a thousand hues, that would have made many a cultivated flower garden blush with envy—numbers of them were new to me—the splendid grass, covering the earth with a luxuriant matting; the clear atmosphere, the pure and bracing breezes sweeping from the gulf, all combined to enchant me with my first Texas spring. And, after all these years, each recurring spring here is as delightful to me as ever; nowhere, in my knowledge, does nature so completely re-invigorate everything and fill everything with new life as it does each spring in Northwest Texas.

H. H. McConnell, *Five Years a Cavalryman*, 1889

THE PUNISHING OF A THIEF NAMED MR. DRAGGLE TAIL

In a frontier country, people are a law unto themselves. . .And the code of honesty is more strict than most people now-a-days imagine. For many years after the organization of Coryell County there was only one reported case of theft and I will relate the circumstances. A party of some eight or ten cow men were hunting stock on Bee House Creek.

A stranger fell in with them, whose name they did not learn, but the cowboys called him "Draggle Tail." He stayed with them in camp that night and next morning a gun was missing, and somehow they all knew that "Draggle Tail" was the guilty man, and when they accused him he was forced to acknowledge his crime and stated that he had hid it during the night with the intention of stealing it.

The gun was found where he located it, and then it was "all off" with Mr. Draggle Tail. They thought he ought to be punished, but did not want to injure him seriously. They also thought he ought to be encouraged to leave the country, as such men were not needed and not allowed to live in Coryell County at that time. After consultation the boys concluded to give him a taste of the cow whip, which in those days consisted of a stock about eighteen inches long, with the heavy plaited whip and lash about fifteen feet long attached, and an experienced hand could split the hide of a cow at every lick.

Mr. Draggle Tail, who rode a good pony, was allowed to select a man out of the crowd to do the whipping and was to have fifteen feet allowance for a start and a chance to go free if he could outrun the cowboy; otherwise he was to take the lash for half a mile every time the cowboy could reach him with the whip.

He selected a man by the name of Thomas Deaton to do the whipping, but Mr. Draggle Tail was very unfortunate in his choice, for Deaton was the most expert man in the crowd with a whip and had a fast horse.

Deaton gave him twenty feet the start and told him to "go." Off they went and about the third jump Deaton's whip split the clothing on his back, a few more licks reached the hide, and when Deaton left him the blood was streaming from his back. Mr. Draggle Tail was never seen nor heard in that county any more.

From a speech by J.H. Crisman, Old Settlers Reunion, Belton, September 4, 1903

"*. . .the most murderous, thieving, gambling, godforsaken hole in the Lone Star State or out of it.*"

An 1845 assessment of Corpus Christi, attributed to Lt. Richard Wilson in *Fifty Years in Camp*, 1909

A FEW TRUTHS OF TEXAS

Texas occupies all of the continent of North America except a small part set aside for the United States, Canada and Mexico. It is bounded on the north by 30-odd states, on the east by all the oceans except the Pacific, on the south by the Texas Border and on the west by the Pacific Ocean and the rest of the world.

Fold Texas northward and Brownsville will be 120 miles into Canada. Fold it eastward and El Paso would be dunked into the Atlantic. Fold it westward and Orange would be 215 miles out in the Pacific. Try it.

Area: 263,644 sq. mi. Water Area: 3,695 sq. mi.

A Texas compass has six directions. North to the Panhandle. South to the Rio Grande. East to East Texas. West to West of the Pecos. Down to Oil. Up to the Texas moon.

North to South: 801 crowflight miles; 918 highway miles.

East to West: 773 crowflight miles; 893 highway miles.

If you flew from Boca Chica, where the Rio Grande empties into the Gulf of Mexico at the southern tip of Texas, to Sabine, where the Sabine River joins the gulf at the Louisiana border, you would fly 328 miles. If you went by highway, you would drive 499 miles. If you started walking every bit of coastline, you would travel over 1,600 miles.

Texas is equal in area to all the New England states plus New Jersey, Delaware, Maryland, Kentucky, South Carolina, West Virginia, Ohio and Indiana with 7,112 square miles left over.

There are 64 counties with greater land area than Rhode Island and there are 254 counties in all.

Texas has 101 peaks over 5,000 feet high and the highest point east of the Rockies is Guadalupe Peak, 8,751 feet high. The town of Sabine Pass is 8 feet above sea level, and Valasco is 11 feet.

There are creek beds that stay dry so much of the time that it is easier to find bird nests in them than fish. There are areas so flat that they have to put signs up to tell the water which way to run when it rains.

John Randolph, *Texas Brags*, 1951

TEXAS EATS

Agarita Jelly

5 1/2 cups agarita juice

7 1/2 cups sugar

1 (1 3/4-ounce) box Sure-Jell

Mix juice and Sure-Jell in a 6-8 quart saucepan. Bring to a boil, stirring constantly. Add sugar quickly and bring to a full rolling boil (a boil that cannot be stirred down), stirring constantly. Remove from heat; skim off foam and quickly pour into sterilized jars or glasses. Cover at once with hot melted paraffin. Cool. Put on lids. Yields about 8 cups.

The agarita is a small, low shrub that grows wild in the Hill Country. The red berries ripen in May. The bush is thorny and it is impossible to gather the berries by hand. The best solution is to spread an old sheet on the ground under the bush. Then with a fairly long stick (I use an old tennis racket), gently beat the bush till the berries fall. You'll have twigs, leaves and insects, too. Remove as many as possible, then wash many, many times. You will need approximately 1 1/2 gallons of berries for the juice. Cook berries with 1 1/2 cups water on medium heat for about 20 minutes. Strain in a jelly bag or through a clean white cloth. If you do not have enough juice, add water to make the correct amount. Don't use more than 1 cup water though.

Another word of advice. Spray yourself well with insect repellent before beating that bush. Chiggers are no fun! Too, be sure none of those long, wiggly creatures are hiding under that bush!

A Texas Hill Country Cookbook, 1978

A LEGAL WEDDING DESPITE THE MISSING COW

Republic of Texas: To all who shall see this present, greeting: Whereas I [Henry Osborne], Clerk of this County, having this morning unthoughtedly tied my office key as a clapper in my cow's bell; and whereas the said cow has gone astray to parts unknown, bearing with her the said key, and therefore the said key is *non inventus est* that is, can't be had: And whereas one Abner Barnes has made application to me for marriage license, and the said Abner persists that he cannot wait until the cow comes back with the key, but is compelled, by the violence of his feelings and the arrangements already made, to get married: Therefore these presents are to command any person legally authorized to celebrate the rites of matrimony to join the said Abner Barnes to Rebecca Downs; and for so doing this shall be your sufficient authority.

Given under my hand and private seal, on the doorstep of my office, the seal of the office being locked up, and my cow having gone away with the key, this fourth day of October, A.D. 1838.

Spirit of the Times, January 23, 1858

A SHORT ASSORTMENT OF JOKES ABOUT TEXAS (BY A YANKEE)

It's one of those typical Texas homes. Even the kitchen has seven rooms.

There's one town in Texas that has so much money that even the Volkswagens are Cadillacs!

I know a fella from Texas who's so rich he just had his gums capped.

I don't care how much money you have—if you want to feel poor, go to a picnic in Texas. Even the paper plates are sterling!

Robert Orben, *The Encyclopedia of One-Line Comedy*, 1966}

★ ★ ★ ★ ★ ★ ★ ★ ★ ★ ★ ★ ★ ★ ★ ★ ★ ★

TEXANESE

Pop skull

In a word: liquor. The cowboy was nothing if not gifted in inventing euphemisms for his drinking materials. Among the others were wild mare's milk, tonsil paint (alternately, tonsil varnish), forty rod, gut warmer, boilermaker and his helper, prairie dew, red disturbance, scamper juice, tanglefoot, Taos lightning, lightning flash, honeydew, jig juice, bumblebee whisky, coffin varnish, conversation fluid, neck oil, forty rod, scorpion Bible, stagger soup, strong water and Brigham Young cocktail.

TEXAS TRAIL DRIVERS STOP TO REST. . .AND DISCOVER ALIENS

We gave several camp dinners for them [rural Kansas settlers]. They would come in their wagons, the girls and all the families. Our cook would outdo himself in getting up all kinds of camp dishes. Our boys would do all kinds of stunts, riding bronco horses and roping, which interested and amused the people. At first they seemed to think we were a bunch of Arabs or outlaws. It was my first contact with real yankee people, and to my surprise, they seemed just about like other people.

A. G. Mills, personal memoirs, 1933

MR. GOODNIGHT RECALLS

"Indians are poor shooters. I reckon I have been shot at and missed more times than any man livin', but I wouldn't say so because nobody would believe me and I wouldn't blame them. There is so much hot air shot about the pioneer days. It's a big nuisance to be an old frontiersman."

Charles Goodnight, legendary Texas rancher, age 90, in the *Fort Worth Star-Telegram*, 1926

HOME FOR CHRISTMAS

When I return home during the Christmas season, I usually spend the first day just standing around in rooms. I peel tangerines while my mother talks about the hometown goings-on; I stare at the same family photographs I have been looking at in the bedroom for the past thirty years; I lean against the fireplace mantel and shell pecans. After dark I stand in the kitchen talking to my father, home from work at his feed store, and having perhaps my sixth or seventh cup of coffee of the day as I listen to my father's often-told tales.

But on the second day I excuse myself from the house about noon and get into the car and take my traditional half-day drive: my simple-minded but satisfying tour through hills and trees and river places. I prepare myself, of course: I select a paperback or two from the grocery bag of books I had put in the trunk for Christmas reading; I stop at a 7-Eleven for a Lone Star and Fritos; and then I ease on down the road toward Medina—the first of the small hill country towns on my itinerary.

It is a rewarding thing to do, this slow driving along the highway.

I munch a Frito, gaze benevolently at the barbed wire of a rancher's fence, thing of. . .damn, just about everything. My thoughts freewheel nicely on that curving farm-to-market road. I notice, I welcome, the steady yellow lines down the center, the silvery shine of metal sign poles, the continuous fence-line posts, the white caliche roads that lead off to hunting cabins and farms. I coast through the mellow browns of winter grasses, pastures, hills—while the sun covers the land like the bright fur of a hibernating animal. Cedars stand along the roadside like friendly country cousins. Midday shadows lie intimately across the road: beguiling, weightless pools.

I feel almost sinfully pleased by such an agreeable home territory. I turn each curve knowing that I can come again in any season and drive along these same roads, gaze into these same fields. I look out my window and I smile: this is my place of worship, my personal museum of art.

In Bandera I go into Hilbrunner's Drug Store and head for the snug little Christmas corner behind the pharmacy—a small counter, three tables, men drinking coffee. I sit at the counter and have hot tea. A rancher sitting next to me is wearing a new leather jacket, new Stetson, thick glasses. I drink my tea and look secretly at the mystery of his large old rancher ears, the red broke veins in the rancher nose. . . .

In Camp Verde I buy a bag of peanuts and another beer and stop for a look at Verde Creek. I get out, walk beneath the trees.

Birds are moving slowly through the cypresses, not singing, flapping their wings heavily: cardinals, woodpeckers, robins down south for the winter. There is no wind, just sunlight coming strongly in an afternoon slant, the clean smell of the creek. Back in the car I pick up *Brighton Rock* and read a little.

In Center Point, just about dusk, in a clear Wyeth-light, I park beside an unplanted field. Beyond the field, several children are still out, idling away the last moments before dark.

But the light, the light. It is ordinary for the hill country, for December, yet as I stand there beside the wire fence, with a windmill rising behind the field, with red and green Christmas bulbs strung around the side windows of nearby houses, with unpaved streets wandering off into the countryside, such light is almost like a voice, a soundless, continuous speaking from the sun-haloed oaks.

Darkness comes; the land shuts down. I drive back toward home, sated, having feasted on cattle guards, creeks, pecan trees, earth.

Elroy Bode, *This Favored Place*, 1983

TEXAS LOST ★ ★ ★ ★ ★ ★ ★ ★
Thank God

Well, actually, "Thank God" never made it as a real town in Texas, but it almost did. That was the suggested name when the railroad finally reached the community along the mid-Texas coast. Cooler heads prevailed, and, possibly because of a strong belief in the separation of church and train, "Thank God" was defeated and the town became Blessing–which it still is in Matagorda County.

[Texas is]. . .a hard, hot, uncompromising landscape, interesting mainly for the bizarre fact that its bushes, instead of standing still as they do in Europe, blow about in the wind; and for its population, which was made up of two mutually hostile races, the Randolphscotts and the Nonrandolphscotts.

Alan Coren, *Punch*, May 1982

I have said that Texas is a state of mind, but I think it is more than that. It is a mystique closely approximating a religion. And this is true to the extent that people either passionately love Texas or passionately hate it and, as in other religions, few people dare to inspect it for fear of losing their bearings in mystery and paradox. Any observations of mine can be quickly canceled by opinion or counter-observation. But I think there will be little quarrel with my feeling that Texas is one thing. For all its enormous range of space, climate, and physical appearance, and for all the internal squabbles, contentions, and strivings, Texas has a tight cohesiveness perhaps stronger than any other section of America. Rich, poor, Panhandle, Gulf, city, country, Texas is the obsession, the proper study and the passionate possession of all Texans.

John Steinbeck, *Travels With Charley*, 1962

How Horses Get Crazy

Once out on the plains up in the Panhandle country, I went to get on a locoed horse, and as I went to mount and caught the cheek of the bridle, he slung me full length of the bridle reins but when I got up, I got on him and rode him. Oh, you take a bad locoed horse, they are really crazy. If you try to drive one over a wagon rut he won't go. Loco is caused from a weed they eat, and the way they get started to eating it is because it's the first weed to come up in the spring and the stock are hungry for something green and they eat it. I have seen big patches of it. It looks just like a pretty turnip patch. It has an effect on stock just like morphine does on people—when they got started they can't quit, they just go wild after it.

Yes, they stay loco as long as they live. The horses are never any account after they once get locoed. When you ride them two or three miles they are give out. I guess there were one-hundred and fifty head of horses out there on that ranch that was locoed.

Once out on the plains I bought a big black horse. His mane and tail was long and wavy just like it had been platted. He wasn't a bad horse and didn't pitch much when I rode him, just reared up, almost fell over backwards with me. He made one of the best saddle horses I ever rode.

About as bad a pitching horse as I ever owned was also a big black horse. He was sure a hard-pitching horse. He pitched about two-hundred yards with me once and when he quit pitching, my hat was off and my heels were in my boot tops. When he quit pitching, my wife says, "Now get off that horse and don't you ever get on him again; let him go with the wild bunch."

But I told her no I was going to ride him to cow camp. Then I got to camp the boys all knew what a bad horse he was and one of them said I didn't ride him. I said, "All right I'll bet you five-hundred dollars I can ride him slick." But he wouldn't call my bet. I rode him all day and worked cattle on him. But I sold him next day, for when he was pitching I kind of lost my eye sight. Everything got dark just like it does when it comes a blue norther. The man I sold him to said he never did pitch with him.

The Library of Congress, WPA Writers Project, from an interview with rancher A.G. Anderson, Uvalde, Texas; undated, but about 1935

TEXAS LOST ★ ★ ★ ★ ★ ★ ★
Zigzag, Texas

What the name meant was that the road leading to this Medina County town was nothing but a long crooked string of zigs and zags. The highway must have been straightened because Zigzag is no more. Interesting: Zigzag must have been located midway between present day Devine and Primitive on FM 2200.

How Snakey Joe Got His Name

Some cowboys were working on the Read Ranch in 1900, which lies in the eastern part of Howard County, where the Rattlesnake and Wild Horse mountains loom against the horizon.

These cowboys were very busy making ready for a fall roundup of several thousand head of three-year old steers and to do some branding of the calves. Red and Joe started to catch their mounts, which were Spanish pintoes.

"Well," said Joe, "where did the wrangler stake our ponies? Look! the hobbles are broken."

Taking his lasso, he started to find his horse. Not watching very carefully where he stepped, he stepped in a prairie dog cell and was bitten by a rattler on the ankle. The warning rattle of the snake did not attract his attention. Not having a first-aid kit with him he gave it a generous dose of tobacco juice, and trusting it to Lady Lack went on his way after his horse.

Becoming tired and worried about his accident, he sat down to meditate upon the situation. However, not noticing where he chose to sit, the mate of the rattler was underneath him. After a few minutes of relaxation, he got up and, deciding that he was not seriously hurt, made another attempt to catch the pony, while the snake, all unknown, dangled from the seat of his trousers.

Finally after a rather strenuous chase, he succeeded in catching the cayuse. Picking his saddle and tossing it on the horse and tightening the girth with a final click, he started to mount, but that was another question. The horse scented the snake and would not stand.

The snake in its mad scramble trying to loose its entangled fangs made itself felt by its weight.

Joe looked around and saw it. "WOW!"

And loudly cursing, he threw up his hands trying to hold the reins in one hand and with the other, locate the trouble, all the while running in circles.

His pal Red stood watching him, dying with laughter, throwing his sombrero in the air, and enjoying the sight. Seeing Joe had almost become exhausted and the frightened horse had begun to trample him, Red made two long jumps and grabbed the snake by one hand, and the horse with the other and separated the trio.

The time had passed and noon-hour had arrived. While seated around the campfire, with the branding irons sizzling in the fire, they were served the famous dish of son-of-a-gun and black coffee as Red related the morning incident.

All eyes and laughter turned toward Joe, crying "Snakey Joe!"

Story related by "Red" Wiggins, 60-year-old "wandering cowboy," November 14, 1936, at Big Spring, Texas, for WPA Writers Project, Library of Congress archives

A RAIL TALE

Back in "those days" a cowboy, drunk and happy, boarded a train in Dallas and gave the conductor a wad of bills.

"Where you bound for?" the conductor asked.

"To hell," answered the cowboy.

"The fare to Fort Worth is $1.50," replied the conductor as he counted out change.

Traditional

THE GUN-PACKERS OF YORE

After leaving Waco [north] the character of the country began to change into a more open prairie, the settlements and farms were further and further apart, and everything bore evidence that we were leaving civilization behind us and approaching the frontier.

I first, at this time [1866] particularly noticed the habit of carrying ("packing" they called it) firearms, new to me then, but soon becoming a familiar sight, and it impressed me as a most useless and dangerous habit, and I have never seen any reason to change my views.

Every man and boy, old and young, rich or poor, at home or abroad, in church, at court, the wedding or the funeral, from the "cradle to the grave," the double-barreled shot gun, or the old-fashioned, brass-mounted dragoon pistol, was inevitably carried by them, and it goes without saying that they all knew how to use them, and did so often without very much provocation.

And yet I cannot look back on the practice as an unmixed evil either, for bar-room brawling, fist fights and minor difficulties were pretty much unknown in those days. The treatment experienced by a bully or a bravado was "short, sharp and decisive;" if he insulted a woman, "took in" a town, or stole a horse, he was shot off-hand by some one, who thereby rendered society a service, at much less expense and without the uncertainty and delay that often attend the law's slow course.

Of course, in the days I write of, the times were more or less out of joint; the civil law was almost a dead letter; the country was filled with the disbanded armies of the collapsed Confederacy, and many of the men returning to find homes destroyed and family ties broken became reckless, if not lawless.

But closer acquaintance with this class of men taught me that often an honest, a brave and noble heart was beating beneath the rough exterior, and that life and property were safer among them than they sometimes are among the "slick" fellows who wear a "boiled" shirt and live in the settlement. The frontiersman, as I saw him then, is rapidly becoming a feature of the past; he is disappearing before the advance of civilization, like the Indian and the buffalo, and I often wonder in my mind whether or not his more cultivated successor possesses the good quality of real nobility to the same extent.

Soon he will be gone forever, passed away, and in the page of romance alone will be found his counterpart. But *he* blazed out the pathway of progress; his log cabin and rawhide door, its puncheon floor and stick chimney are gone; *he* made the *present* possible.

H.H. McConnell,
Five Years a Cavalryman, 1889

★ ★ ★ ★ ★ ★ ★ ★ ★ ★ ★ ★ ★ ★ ★ ★ ★

Of the 59 signers of the 1836 Texas Declaration of Independence
. . .only 2 were native Texans,
. . .only 1 was among Stephen Austin's original settlers
. . .only 10 had lived in Texas for more than six years
. . .only 17 had been in Texas more than six months

Source: Louis Wiltz Kemp,
The Signers of the Texas Declaration of Independence, 1944

THE COW THAT FELL IN THE DUGOUT

"Yes, a cow fell into my house," said J. G. Hardin, with a chuckle. "I'll tell you how it happened. The family was snug and warm, safe from the winds and lightening storms in our dugout in 1879 [west of Wichita Falls].

"The dugout was fine-timbered and lined. It needed a door, however, and while I was making the door one of those Texas blizzards blew up with several inches of snow.

"A good cattleman takes care of his cattle, so I spread a wagon sheet over the doorway and went to work on a shed for the cattle just outside the shack. This was soon covered with snow but it was a break from the wind.

"I went into the house to get warm.

"In the shed the mules got to fighting for a good warm place, crowding out the cows. I couldn't blame them much; Brrr! That wind was keen.

"But one old cow just couldn't take it. She broke out and ran across the prairie. That was bad enough in such weather as that, but when she chose her path across the dugout entrance it was just too bad for every one concerned.

"Talk about unexpected company dropping in! Well there she was, wagon sheet, snow, and all. Of course we all hollered. That scared her and away she went out of the dugout, scampering away over the prairie again with the wagon sheet on her horns. Provoked as I was I had to laugh as I chased that fool cow."

The Library of Congress,
WPA Writers Project,
Interview with rancher J.G. Hardin, 1937

SMILE WHEN YOU CALL ME THAT

When we hear a man say "Texan," we involuntarily look to see if he has the lock-jaw, or if he has ice in his mouth. There is no excuse for a man to use such a word in a mild climate. The genius of our language requires generally the termination "ian," when it is necessary to give a name to the inhabitants of that country. "Texian" is the name for which we fought, and which shows ourselves independent of all foreign dictation. Let us stand up for the rights of the 'old Texian' against the ruthless Goths and Vandals who are endeavoring to deprive him of that which has blazed to brilliantly from the folds of his banner over all his battle-fields.

From a debate over the etymological correctness of the use of "Texan" vs "Texian," The Texas Monument, February 5, 1851

★ ★ ★ ★ ★ ★ ★ ★ ★ ★ ★ ★ ★ ★ ★ ★

MR. GOODNIGHT, THE ANTHROPOLOGIST

"You know, the Kiowas were really Eskimos. They came down in sleds drawn by dogs and once in Texas they joined the Comanches."

Charles Goodnight, legendary Texas rancher, age 90, quoted in the Fort Worth Star-Telegram, 1926

STAGE ROBBERY

Texas, of course, had its stage coaches and, therefore, its share of the stagecoach hold-ups. The hold-up I now have in mind occurred in Llano County, near the town of Llano in the year of 1883. The passengers were Miss Jennie Todd. . .Miss Cora Bridges . . .and G.W. Todd. They were returning from Austin after having spent several days in the city. They were only a short distance outside the town of Llano, and it was about two o'clock p.m. The stage-driver was in good spirits, and the horses were fresh and going at their usual speed. . .

The two masked robbers jumped from the bushes, one of them grabbing the lead horse by the bridle. The other threw his gun on the driver and commanded him to halt. The passengers being inside thought nothing of the sudden stop, thinking the driver was picking up another passenger, and began to make room for him. Then the robber jerked the stage door open and ordered them to "get out." They promptly gratified his desire.

Misses Jennie Todd and Cora Bridges began to cry. One of the robbers held his pistol in Mr. Todd's face while the other searched him. The girls, of course, continued their crying, and Mr. Todd said to them, "Girls, be quiet; these 'gentlemen' won't hurt you." (Mr. Todd said he was very particular to say "gentlemen.") A moment later he repeated to the girls what he had said, and one of the robbers, apparently resenting such a mild insinuation, pointed the cocked gun a little closer, and said: "You shut up, old man, or we will bore a hole through you!" Mr. Todd kept quiet. The robbers did not disturb the girls, and their hold-up only netted them a watch and chain and $3.85 in change from Mr. Todd.

They continued their journey to the next stage stand. . . The robbers were captured the following day. Each of them was sentenced for 25 years in the Federal prison.

Mrs. A.W. Kooch of Austin, *Frontier Times*, July 1927

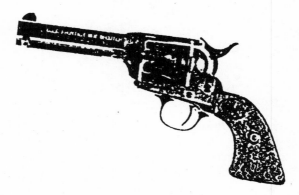

A BRIT EXPLAINS TEXAS' PLACE IN THE UNIVERSE

When Alaska achieved statehood Texas did not for a moment surrender its historic place in the grammar of American language and braggadocio; big, bigger, biggest, Texan. Texans argue that while Alaska is twice as large in terms of crude bulk it is Texas that remains, in more significant ways, powerful, grand and pre-eminent, the basic American metaphor for size, grossness, power, wealth, ambition, high-rolling, and boasting: in a word, Texanic.

Texas is a great geographic, geological and human confluence. Its configuration, roughly that of a horn of plenty, is celebrated in Texas-shaped bathmats, fruitcakes, ice cubes, key rings, buckles, spectacle frames, stationery, jewelry, and soap. It is the dominant state of the main body of the United States. Covering 267,338 square miles, it is larger than France, larger than Spain, more than twice the area of Italy, nearly three times larger than Britain. The 800-mile length of Texas is the same distance as that between London and the Faeroes, and between Paris and Naples. The state is almost as broad as it is long and the people talk of being on Texas Standard Time.

Texans believe themselves to be both the distillers and guardians of the holy American stuff, the mystical, original raw spirit they fear has vanished in other sucked-out parts of the country—a keen devotion to the rumbustious, vigorous and unhindered pursuit of wealth. Isn't this, they ask, what America is for? Does not free-wheeling capitalism constitute freedom's fortress? Isn't this what American democracy and ideas of liberty are predicated on?

Trevor Fishlock, *The State of America*, 1986

HELL IS A TWO-SIDED COIN

Money, or lack of it, was the least of the cowboy's worries; independence and the dignity of his vocations was all. He was a horseman, which gave him pride. . . His string of saddle horses was his utmost concern—for without a good mount, a good cowboy is no cowboy at all. If he could find a paying job, what the hell! And if he couldn't, what the hell!

John L. Sinclair, *Cowboy Riding Country*, 1982

TEXAS EATS

Fried Chicken

It is doubtful if any dish is as over-exposed or as poorly presented as. . .fried chicken. It can be one of the tastiest methods of preparing chicken, or it can be a complete flop. Real southern fried chicken is not loaded with a heavy crust, but has only a thin crust of flour, is very tender, moist, and cooked through and through.

The following recipe is my method of cooking Southern Fried Chicken—or the Texas method.

Use young fryers 1 1/2 to 2 pounds each. One such fryer should serve 4 persons generously. Wash the chickens thoroughly and pat dry with paper towels. Cut into serving pieces and sprinkle each with salt and pepper. Dredge in flour, or shake the pieces in a paper bag containing flour, salt, and pepper. In a heavy skillet with fitting lid, heat fresh vegetable shortening; never use leftover fat. The fat should be about 2 to 3 inches deep in the skillet after it has melted. Let the fat heat to the sizzling point but not to the smoking point. Drop in the pieces and fry for 5 or 6 minutes, turning at least once, then reduce the heat slightly. Cover with a heavy lid and continue frying at a constant heat without having the heat near the burning point. Turn as necessary to brown on all sides. When the pieces are brown and fork-tender, remove the lid and continue cooking just a few minutes longer, turning once more to dry and crisp the outside. Drain on brown paper and serve.

Sara Morgan, *The Saga of Texas Cookery*, 1973

*I did know one feller that had killed three men. . .*Bud Knolles, it was. He killed his first one up at Batson during the oil boom, but there was so many killed up there that if it wasn't a plain case of murder, the authorities didn't even arrest them for it. That's what happened to Bud.

The next one he killed was when they was building the Missouri Pacific railroad from Beaumont to Houston. Him and another mule-skinner got in an argument, and that evening after they come in and tended to their teams, they each got a singletree and got after each other. Bud got beat up some but finally split the feller's head open and then finished him off on the ground. They took that one to the grand jury, but they no-billed him on self-defense.

The third was at Liberty. Him and somebody—I can't remember his name right off—had a falling out at the saloon and just fell out in the street with their pocket knives and cut each other down and then laid side by side and kept cutting til they was drug apart. Bud finally got over it, but the other feller died. They no-billed him on that'un, too.

Well, after that lots of folks was skeered of Bud, and he knowed it and got pretty overbearing, 'specially when he'd had a few drinks. People would get out of his way and leave him alone all they could and try to get along any way they could, and he just got worse and worse.

Well, he come to town one day and hit several saloons and was coming out of one just as old Cap'n Nance was going in, and Bud just pushed the old man down on the porch and told him to get the hell out of the way and went on.

Now, if there ever was a mild man, it was the old captain. He'd fought from start to finish in the Civil War, and when he came back, he bought a place a mile or two out of town and settled down to minding his own business and leaving other folks alone, unless he was needed. He'd got too old to farm— he was ever' bit of eighty—but he'd walk into town every day, get the mail and one drink, and go back home. That's what he done after Bud pushed him down. Got his drink and went home.

Well, sir, I heard he got some water and cooled awhile and then took a bucket and some other things and went out next to the road and set down on the bucket in a little patch of brush under a big tree. Directly he got up and cut a sprout and set back down and whittled on it while he was waiting.

Just before sundown he heard a horse coming and leaned forward and jabbed the stick in the ground. It was forked, and he laid his old double-barrel on it, and when Bud Knolles got close on the road as he was coming, the captain cut him half in two with one barrel, and when Bud's horse run off and the dust settled, he took his time and walked over and give him the other barrel.

I learnt two things out of that. One is that when they said Colonel Colt made all men equal, they didn't give near enough credit to Mr. Remington's ole double-barrels, and the other'n was that old folks don't like to be pushed around any more than young ones do.

Bill Brett, *This Here's a Good'un*, 1983

HOUSTON IN 1839
Number of houses: 382
Population: 3,000
Number of women: 40
Number of businesses: 65
Number of saloons: 47

Edward Stiff, *The Texan Emigrant*, 1840

TEXAS POETICAL

A Prayer for a Cowboy

My Dear Brethern and Sisters,
We've gathered here today,
To try and give our last respects
To a friend who passed away.

Now we all know he had some faults
To make a preacher frown,
But you must remember he's a cowboy,
And I'm not here to tear him down.

He spent his life out in the hills.
He felt that God was there.
It didn't matter how hard the task.
He always did his share.

He never harmed a neighbor
Nor cheated on a friend.
If a man would help himself,
He stayed with him to the end.

He never misused horses.
He had no greed or hate.
If he rode through your pasture,
He would always close the gate.

But now he's gone to meet his Maker
In the land up in the sky.
Where I hope he has good horses,
And springs are never dry.

I hope he has a bedroll
Where he'll be warm at night.
He'll need that same old happy heart
And that same old smile so bright.

I don't think he cares to play a harp
Up there in the heavenly choir.
Just let him have some old cow hide
To while away the hour.

But let him have some cattle
With calves to rope and brand.
I know if you do this, dear Lord,
He'll try to make a hand.

He wouldn't ask this much for himself,
But he is our 'dear friend.'
Just treat him like he treated us;
That's all we ask—Amen.

Van Holyoak, *The Cowboy and the Horse*, 1976

"DOG FACE" RIDES HIS FIRST TRAIN HOME FROM DODGE CITY

Old "Dog Face" Smith was a typical Texan, about thirty years of age, with long hair and three months growth of whiskers. He wore a blue shirt and a red cotton handkerchief around his neck. He had a bright intelligent face that bore the appearance of a good trail hound, which no doubt was the cause of people calling him "Dog Face". . .

I will never forget seeing that train come into Dodge City that night. Old "Dog Face" and his bunch were pretty badly frightened, and we had considerable difficulty in getting them aboard. It was about 12:30 when the train pulled out. The conductor came around, and I gave him my cowboy ticket. It was almost as long as your arm, and as he tore off a chunk of it I said: "What authority have you to tear up a man's ticket?" He laughed and said, "You are on my division. I simply tore off one coupon and each conductor between here and San Antonio will tear off one for each division." That sounded alright, but I wondered if that ticket would hold out all the way down.

Everyone seemed to be tired and worn out and the bunch began bedding down. . . At about three o'clock our train was sidetracked to let the westbound train pass. This little stop caused the boys to sleep the sounder. Just then the westbound train sped by traveling at the rate of about forty miles an hour and just as it passed our coach the engineer blew the whistle. Talk about your stampedes! That bunch of sleeping cowboys arose as one man, and started on the run with old "Dog Face" Smith in the lead. I was a little slow in getting off, but fell in with the drags. I had not yet woke up, but thinking I was in a genuine stampede, yelled out, "Circle your leaders and keep up the drags!" Just then the leaders circled and ran into the drags, knocking some of us down. They circled again and the butcher [food vendor] crawled out from under foot and jumped through the window like a frog. Before they could circle back the next time, the train crew pushed in the door and caught old "Dog Face" and soon the bunch quieted down. The conductor was pretty angry and threatened to have us transferred to the freight department and loaded onto a stock car.

Jack Potter, quoted in *The Trail Drivers of Texas*, 1925

★ ★ ★ ★ ★ ★ ★ ★ ★ ★ ★ ★ ★ ★ ★ ★ ★ ★ ★

An average cattle drive in 1880 was made up of:

★ *2,500/3,000 head of cattle*
★ *60 horses*
★ *1 trail boss*
★ *8 cowboys (drovers)*
★ *1 horse wrangler*
★ *1 cook*
★ *1 chuck wagon*

A TEXAN DISCOVERS THE WHEEL

Old Martin Varner used to tell a story of his little son's first experience with a biscuit. The old man had managed to get together enough money or pelts to buy a barrel of flour. Mrs. Varner made a batch of biscuits, which, considering the resources of the country, were doubtless heavy as lead and hard as wood. When they were done, Mrs. Varner set them on the table. The boy looked at them curiously, helped himself to one, and made for the door with it. In a few minutes he came back for another. Doubting the child's ability to eat it so quickly, the old man followed him to see what disposition he made of the second. The ingenious youngster had conceived a novel and not altogether illogical idea of their utility. He had punched holes through the center, inserted an axle and triumphantly displayed a miniature Mexican cart. And I assure you, from my recollection of those pioneer biscuits they were capable of sustaining a pretty heavy load.

Noah Smithwick, *The Evolution of a State*, 1900

★ ★ ★ ★ ★ ★ ★ ★ ★ ★ ★ ★ ★ ★ ★ ★ ★ ★ ★

A MODEST CLAIM. . . .

Perhaps no other country in the world with as small a population as that of Texas can boast of so large a percentage of thoroughly, scientifically and liberally educated men of the upper and middle classes as can Texas.

Viktor Friederich Bracht, *Texas in 1848*, 1931

. . . .ON THE OTHER HAND

The inhabitants in general are. . .composed of a class who had been unfortunate in life; as it could hardly be supposed that the fortunate. . .would voluntarily make a choice of Texas.

David Barnett Edward, *The History of Texas, or, The Emigrant's, Farmer's, and Politician's Guide*, 1836

THE SIX-SHOOTER BEATS THE 20-SHOOTER

Imagine a battle between the Texans and the Comanches before the advent of the six-shooter. The Texan carried at most three shots, the Comanche carried two score or more arrows. It took the Texan a minute to reload his weapon; the Indian in that time could ride three hundred yards and discharge twenty arrows. The Texan had to dismount in order to use his rifle effectively at all, and it was his most reliable weapon; the Indian remained mounted throughout the combat. Apparently the one advantage possessed by the white man was a weapon of longer range and more deadly accuracy than the Indian's bow, but the agility of the Indian and the rapidity of his movements did much to offset this advantage.

Walter Prescott Webb, *The Texas Rangers*, 1935

Terrorist Turkeys Mug Rattlesnakes; Deer, Hogs, Roadrunners Cheer Them On

Rattlesnakes were found in great numbers in west Texas, and they were enemies that had to be guarded against at all times. Wild turkeys always show a great antipathy to them and never fail to make a deadly and persistent attack until the reptile is destroyed. . .

I was traveling the road near Uvalde when I saw a large flock of wild turkeys in an open glade near the highway. I stopped when I saw the gobblers had congregated in a circle, where they seemed to be fighting, but I soon perceived they were killing a large rattlesnake. One after the other would spring into the air in rapid succession and come down on the reptile, which they struck a hard blow with one wing that might have been heard quite a distance. Apparently all the gobblers took part in the fracas, and they appeared to be greatly excited, but the hens fed quietly in the vicinity and seemed to be indifferent to what was going on.

I watched them about ten minutes before they observed my presence and became alarmed. After they disappeared in the brush I approached the place and found the snake coiled up and almost dead. Evidently the gobblers had been engaged in killing him for some time before I appeared on the scene, and if they had not been disturbed the victim would have provided a feast for the whole flock because it is their custom to eat the snakes, killed in that way.

Deer are equally prejudiced against rattlesnakes and invariably attack them in favorable localities. . . The deer springs from a safe distance into the air with his four feet brought together, and he comes down on the snake with his sharp pointed hoofs, which cut like a knife. The movements are rapid and often repeated until the rattler is mangled into a shapeless mass.

The Javelina or Mexican wild hog, found in many parts of Texas. . .will also kill and eat them, and so does a chaparral cock [roadrunner].

August Santleben, *A Texas Pioneer*, 1910

Murder and Justice in Houston

March 22/1838. Fine day—criminals whip[ped] at the post—Jones convicted of murder. A plainer case than which has seldom been submitted to a jury.

March 23/1838. Quick convicted of murder—a case similar to Jones'. Killed Mandord Wood, a Bro. of Ferdinando and Benj. Wood, N.Y.—Quick a savage blood thirsty, malicious looking devil. Grand Jury discharged after having presented 270 indictments, 4 for murder, 4 treason, 8 arson, 40 larceny—the Bar gave a supper to the Grand Jury—high meeting, some gloriously drunk.

March 24/1838. Judge Robertson sentenced John Quick and James Jones to be hung on Wednesday next between the hours of 10 & 2 p.m.—an excellent sentence.

March 25/1838. All peaceable—a dreaded reform in the morals of Houston.

March 26/1838. Jones the Convict attempted to kill himself by shooting but shot over his head.

March 28/1838. A delightful day, worthy of other deeds—140 men order'd out to guard the Criminals to the gallows—a concourse of from 2,000 to 3,000 persons on the ground and among the whole not a single sympathetic tear was dropped—Quick addressed the crowd in a stern composed & hardened manner entirely unmoved up to the moment of swinging off the cart—Jones seemed frightened altho' as hardened in crime as Quick—They swung off at 2 o'clock p.m. and were cut down in 35 minutes, not having made the slightest struggle.

J. H. Herdon, diary, 1837-1838

The Lure of Lubbock

This here cowboy, my old pal, Pink Robertson, dreamed he died and went to heaven. (This is a dream!) The arrival of a Texas cowboy was such an unusual event that Saint Peter [took him] to a half dozen men staked out like unbroken broncs. The cowboy faced Saint Peter inquiringly.

"Yes, we're still in heaven," replied the Saint.

"Then why in hell," exclaimed the old boy from the North Plains, "do you have these here men all staked out?"

"Well," said Saint Peter, with a slight attempt to restrain his impatience, "them are all cowboys from the Panhandle of Texas. If we turn 'em loose, the rascals will every last one go back."

Traditional

★ ★ ★ ★ ★ ★ ★ ★ ★ ★ ★ ★ ★ ★ ★ ★ ★ ★

A Texas Truth

". . .[H]ere in Texas, [the men] do not have any pleasure. When they come together sometime, what do they? They can only sit all around the fire and speet! Why, then they drink some whisky; or may be they play cards, or they make great row. They have no pleasure as in Germany."

Why, then did he come to Texas?

"Because here I am free."

A German settler explaining Texas to Frederick Law Olmsted, *A Journey Through Texas*, 1857

TEXAS POETICAL

Bob Sears' Chili Joint

There's a smell about good chili
That no poet can portray;
* It wafts a rare aroma*
Where the gentle breezes play;
* And of all exotic odors*
That the wings-of-time anoint,
* There's none can match description*
With Bob Sears' Chili Joint

Now it wasn't much to look at,
Just a hole there in the wall,
* No sign above the entrance*
And no fancy front atall.
* A stranger couldn't find it*
'Less the wind was blowin' right;
* Then he couldn't hardly miss it,*
Even on the darkest night.

A dime would buy a bowl full
Of that wondrous bill-of-fare;
* A quarter got a milk shake*
And another bowl to spare.
* It wasn't always fresh and clean*
By sanitation's letter,
* But somehow it improved with age*
And day by day got better.

I've eaten Antoine's Crepe Suzettes,
A joy beyond compare;
* I've dined at old Delmonico's,*
Where famed gourmets repair;
* But no Chef has ever challenged*
That high gastronomic point
* That was mine in early childhood*
In Bob Sears' Chili Joint.

Carlos Ashley, Sr., Texas poet laureate, 1949-1951,
That Spotted Sow and Other Texas Hill Country Ballads, 1975

[Monsieur] Violet developed a special hatred for public officials in Texas. In Austin [1840s] he saw them under "their true colors." Every evening, about five o'clock, almost all of them, including the President of the republic, the secretaries, judges, ministers, and members of Congress, were more or less tipsy. In the quarrels which ensued never a night passed without four or five stabbings or shootings. If the Texans were in their usual form, the riot continued during the major portion of the night. . . [A] friend cautioned him, too, that a visitor who passed even a few days among "the gallant members of Congress" should not be surprised if he missed his holsters, his stirrups, his blankets, or even one of his horses. Violet cut short his stay in Austin accordingly. . .

We have no way of knowing how M. Violet affected the Texans he scorned, but the chances are good that they considered his name appropriate.

Joseph Leach, *The Typical Texan*, 1952

**"*Many Texas towns*
are too small to support
one lawyer, but none is
too small to support
two lawyers."**

Attributed to Lyndon Johnson,
quoted in *Texas Wit and Wisdom*,
Wallace Chariton, 1990

A SUPERLATIVE ROOSTIN' PLACE

TEXAS EATS

The trail from Boquillas, Coahuila north into the United States [Big Bend] has been in use since Indian times. There has been many horse thieves, soldiers and outlaws, both American and Mexican, that have used it since back in the '80s. The Indians used it centuries before that. I have followed the tracks of stolen cattle and horses that were taken down the trail. Some of them I caught, some got across the Rio Grande into Mexico.

McKinney Springs, the only water on the trail for over 60 miles, still runs clear and cold. The deer, panther, bobcats, javelina, coyotes and blue quail still water there, as they have for thousands of years. I have laid down on my belly on top of their tracks and drank the cold water countless times. Many a time, I have rolled out of my bedroll and spent the night in absolute solitude with no sound except [my horse] "Old Red" eating the bunch grass, and now and then, a coyote barking. The drumming of the blue quail will wake you up at daylight, and occasionally a panther coming in for water will cause a little disturbance if you have hobbled your horse too close to the water. I don't know of any place on earth where the air is cleaner and the moon shines brighter than the McKinney Mountain area in Big Bend National Park. I don't blame the Indians for fighting for country like that. If I owned it, I would be damn hard to root out of there. There are graves beside the trail that attest to the fact that all that rode over it didn't make it. But I don't know of a better place to roost now. I like the sound of the desert wind, the sounds of the wildlife, and I like to hear the owls hoot.

C.M. "Buck" Newsome, retired border patrolman, *Shod With Iron*, 1975

One identification of West Texas is simply that it is dry. Dryness creates a way of life more demanding than the facts of heat or height or abnormal wetness. The too dry region is hardest to accommodate by man because he is the thirstiest animal. Even when he is trying to adjust to dry living he sometimes consumes more water than he has any right to. This is one of the ways in which rainfall influenced the history of West Texas. Up to the 1870s even the occasional scientific expert who wandered around it thought most of the area as uninhabitable. It was too dry for crops and humans. As one of the early Army officers reported, "This country will be unsuited to human use for a hundred years, if then anyone wants it."

A.C. Greene, *A Personal Country*, 1969

Boiled Collard Greens

Many East Texans save the pot liquor from cooked greens as a soup base or use it as a dunk for cornbread.

3 pounds fresh young collard greens

1 pound salt pork or bacon

1 1/2 cups water

1 teaspoon sugar

Salt and black pepper

Strip the leaves of the greens from their stems and wash them in several changes of cold water to remove all traces of dirt.

Cut the salt pork or bacon into pieces and fry them in a heavy skillet over moderate heat, stirring frequently, until crisp. Transfer the meat and drippings to a bowl and pour the 1 1/2 cups water into the hot skillet. Bring the water to a boil over high heat while scraping loose any brown meat particles that cling to the bottom and sides of the pan. Remove from heat and set aside.

Place the greens in a large, heavy pot and set over high heat. Cover tightly and cook until the greens begin to wilt (about 3-4 minutes). Stir in the meat and drippings, the skillet liquid, and the sugar. Cover and continue cooking over moderate heat until the greens are tender (about 45 minutes).

Drain off the liquid and season the greens with as much salt and pepper as you like.

Elizabeth Davis & Laurie Strickland-Hays, *Southern Seasons, An Authentic Guide to Traditional East Texas Cooking,* 1986

A TEXAS WELFARE STORY

A Texas millionaire went into a church to pray. He knelt and said:

"O Lord, I know everything has to operate according to your will. But I understand you listen to prayers, so here I am. First, Lord, I want to tell you about my ranch out in the hill country. It's not a great big spread, just three thousand cows in my foundation herd, good white-faced stuff. It's getting pretty dry up there, and if it don't rain in a couple of weeks, I'll have to start feeding. So if you could send a rain that way, I sure would appreciate it.

"Then, Lord, I bought some land up in Colorado. Supposed to be uranium land, but I don't know how it'll turn out. But if you could let it turn out good, I sure would be grateful.

"Then, Lord, I've got sixteen oil wells drilling. Of course, Lord, everybody knows that a man can't expect to get oil in every wildcat he drills, and I'm not asking for oil in all sixteen. But, Lord, if you could let me have oil in twelve, I'd sure be obliged to you, Amen."

While the oilman was praying, a man in a threadbare suit had entered quietly and taken a seat. He now knelt to pray. He said, "O, Lord, I've done everything I know to do, and I don't know anything else to do but pray. I'm an accountant, and I lost my job when the firm sold out to another company. That was six months ago, and my savings are all gone. It's hard for a man forty-seven years old to find a new job, but I've tried. I've worn out my shoes going from one place to another. Then my suit is beginning to look shabby, and I have a wife in the hospital. The doctor says she can go home, but I owe the hospital a hundred and seventy dollars and they won't let her go. And every day they add twelve dollars to the bill. O Lord, please help me in some way to get on my feet again. Amen."

The oilman pulled out his wallet and peeled off five one-hundred-dollar bills and quietly placed them in the accountant's hand. Then he knelt again and said, "Lord, you needn't bother about this little chicken—I've taken care of him."

B.A. Bodkin, *A Treasury of Western Folklore*, 1975

★ ★ ★ ★ ★ ★ ★ ★ ★ ★ ★ ★ ★ ★ ★ ★ ★ ★ ★

THE TEXAS HOMESTEAD LAW IS

. . .the bulwark of the home owner and husbandman. It has enhanced the meaning of the word 'home' for him, his wife, and children. In Texas more than any other place in the world, the house of the toiler, or the aggressive farmer, is his castle, and though he live or die, succeed or fail, the faithful woman who has worked with him, and the tiny baby in her arms, will be defended and nourished by the strong laws which were made and are enforced in their behalf.

South and West Land Company,
The Last of the Great Prairie Farming Lands, 1906

TEXAS POETICAL

Far, Far West

When life is over and my race is run,
When death shadows gather and
　　my time has come,
When I've rode my last horse and have
　　turned my last steer,
When my soul has winged its way to that
　　celestial sphere,
When my grave has been dug and I've
　　been laid to rest,
Please let it be in the far, far West.

J.E. McCauley, Seymour, Texas, 1924

I had once doubted the existence of those mythical beings called 'Nature's Noblemen,' but my stay in Texas relieved my mind from all uncertainty on the subject, for I found no lack of polish and courtesy, although the country is so newly settled.

Teresa Griffin Viele, *Following the Drum*, 1858

Funeral of the Heroes of the Alamo

In conformity with an order from the General, commanding the army at headquarters, Colonel John N. Seguin, with his command, stationed at Bexar paid honors of war to the remains of the heroes of the Alamo.

The ashes were found in three places. The two smallest heaps were carefully collected, placed in a coffin, neatly covered with black and having the names of Travis, Bowie, and Crockett engraved on the inside of the lid, and carried to Bexar and placed in the parish church, where the Texian flag, a rifle, and a sword were laid upon it for the purpose of being accompanied by the procession, which was formed at three o'clock on the 25th of February, 1837.

The honors to be paid were announced in order of the previous evening, and by the tolling knell from daybreak to the hour of interment. . . The procession then proceeded to the principal spot, the place of interment, where the graves had been prepared [and] the coffin placed on the principal heap of ashes.

Colonel Seguin made the following address in his native tongue, Castilian:

"Companions in arms, these hallowed relics which we now have the melancholy task of bearing onward, to consign to their kindred earth, are all that remain of those heroic men who so nobly fell, valiantly defending yon tower of the Alamo. If they, my brave associates, preferred rather to die a thousand times than basely bow under the vile yoke of tyranny, what a brilliant, what an illustrious example have they bequeathed us. How worthy to illumine with unchanging splendor the ever glowing pages of history. Even now the genius of liberty is looking down from her lofty seat, smiling with approbation upon our proceedings and calling to us in the names of departed brethren, Travis, Bowie and Crockett, and their iron hearted band, bids us in imitating their mighty deeds to secure like them a high place upon the scroll of immortality.

"Since then, soldiers and fellow citizens, undying fame is the glorious reward of those who fall in this noble contest; cheerfully will I encounter the most formidable dangers which fortune can crown in the path of glory in the noble attempt to achieve my country's independence, regardless of whatever indignity the brutal ferocity of my enemies may have to offer to my lifeless body. I would joyfully perish on the field of battle shouting the war cry, 'God and Liberty, Victory or Death,' of these heroes."

Thus have the last rites of a Christian burial been performed over these brave men. In after times when peace shall have returned to smile upon our prosperous country, a towering fabric of architecture shall be reared by their grateful countrymen above their ashes, designating Bexar as the monument city of Texas, where long after the massive walls of the Alamo have crumbled into dust, the votaries of freedom shall yearly assemble to celebrate at this "TOMB of HEROES" the mighty achievements of the unreturning brave.

Lance Parker, reporting in the *Republic of Texas News*, March 27, 1837. The exact burial site is not now known.

119

How Texas Cowboys Played "Pulling the Chicken"

A lusty young rooster was procured and three hundred yards below town the fun opened. The rooster was buried in the earth, his head only being left above ground, and the young men and boys who wished to participate in this part of the programme were mounted and gathered about. . . Then they dash by, one after another, and as they pass the rooster each man swings himself down from the saddle and reaches for its head. The chicken naturally dodges more or less and renders it no easy matter to catch him. Finally secured, however, by the lucky grab, the body is brought out by a jerk which generally breaks the neck, and the horseman, chicken in hand, dashes away at his best speed, all the rest giving chase for the possession of the rooster. If another overtakes him and wrests it from him, then he leads the race until someone else can take it.

The Tascosa Pioneer, July 31, 1886

"How to Conquer Texas Before Texas Conquers Us"

Pamphlet title, Edward Everett Hale, circa 1855

Have you ever wondered why, at old pioneer home sites in Texas, there is always a cedar tree planted near the front. A few reasons:

1. Makes ironing easier by using wax from running a hot iron over a sprig of cedar.

2. Lay fans of cedar between clothes stored in wardrobes and drawers to repel insects and freshen clothes.

3. Used as air freshener for damp houses.

4. Decorations for Christmas season.

5. Use cedar fans to cool yourself and switch away insects while sitting on the porch.

6. Also used for medicinal purposes.

Attributed to Velma Price Hall, quoted in *A Pinch of This and a Handful of That*, 1898

★ ★ ★ ★ ★ ★ ★ ★ ★ ★ ★ ★ ★ ★ ★ ★ ★ ★

AND A GOOD THING, TOO

I worked around cattle all my life, and I guess I learned all there is to know about it, and I think I can sum it all up in one thing: You can't drink coffee on a running horse. . .

Samuel Brenner, Lubbock, Texas, 1962

GRANNY'S LAMENT

This sweep of shortgrass country [Texas Panhandle] is the old buffalo plains, where the wind blows free, where the altitude ranges in a northwestward slope from 1600 to 4600 feet above sea level, and where the average rainfall is only slightly more than twenty inches.

The region was the last in Texas to be hit by hordes of homesteaders because it was high and dry, with little wood and water and almost no protection from the blue northers that whistled across the wide-open spaces.

You can see the whole development of the high plains in the story of one girl's life. She was a beautiful young lady with golden hair, as luscious as a ripe peach. She married a man who had pioneering in his veins, and they rolled out by wagon to the high plains, almost against the New Mexico line. There they started life in a sod-thatched dugout with only prairie dogs as neighbors.

Eventually, after several children had arrived, they built a little house with two wind-blown locust trees out front. By this time there was a scatter of neighbors, and these pioneers stuck close to home. Anyone who had been over to Carlsbad in New Mexico to see the cavern had really been somewhere.

In the course of time the golden-haired bride became a grandmother, and she was called Granny. She was the mainstay of the family. She could do anything. If a dollar were needed, Granny could find one deep in her purse—butter and egg money.

One day Granny became ill and couldn't get out of bed. All the members of the family went to pieces, for this had never happened before. They simply couldn't manage without Granny, so they hurriedly called the doctor.

As he examined her, he said, "You've been through menopause, haven't you, Granny?"

"Lord, no," she said. "I ain't even been through Carlsbad Cavern. I ain't been anywhere except right here."

Lewis Nordyke, *The Truth About Texas*, 1957

✪ ✪ ✪ ✪ ✪ ✪ ✪ ✪ ✪ ✪ ✪ ✪ ✪ ✪ ✪ ✪ ✪ ✪ ✪

LEGEND OF THE PECAN

The Kiowas have a legend about the origin of the pecan:

Many, many years ago, the Great White Father lived among them on the Great Plains. They were a happy people, for the Great White Father had led them in many triumphant battles against their enemies. He had also brought them good fortune on their hunts. But the time came when he told them he had to leave them to go to the spirit world. The Indians took the body and buried it in a stream bed, covering it carefully with rocks. All the Kiowas looked upon the grave as a sacred place. One time, some of the men, when paying a visit to the grave, noticed a small green plant coming out of the site. They nurtured the plant, knowing it was sacred. After many years, nuts began to fall from the tree, and from these nuts, other trees grew until there were many, many trees bearing the delicious nuts. This was the pecan, an Indian word meaning "nut," which the Kiowas regarded as their special gift from the Great White Father.

Eats, A Folk History of Texas Foods,
Ernestine Linck and Joyce Roach, 1989

*Four stores, four whores,
and a syrup mill.*

Traditional, the comical makeup
of any backwoods East Texas village

THE SALT WAR: MOB MURDERS IN EL PASO

Then [John] Atkinson and [Frank] McBride were led out and stood on the spot where [District Judge Charles] Howard had died. McBride said nothing. Atkinson spoke in excellent Spanish. . .

The crowd shouted, *"Acabanlos! acabanlos!"* ("Finish them! finish them!")

"Then," said Atkinson, "there is no remedy."

The crowd shouted, "No! No!"

"Then," said Atkinson, "let me die with honor. I will give the word." He took off his coat and vest and opened his shirt to bare his breast and looked at the eight men with guns ready to fire and said in his calm manner: "When I give the word, fire at my heart. . . .Fire!"

As he gave the word five bullets struck him in the belly. He staggered but recovered himself and shouted: *"Mas arriba, cabrones!"* ("Higher, you bastards!") Two more shots were fired and he fell but was still not dead. He motioned to his head and Desiderio Apodaca, the commander of the firing party, put a pistol to his head and finished him. McBride was instantly killed and the bodies were dragged off. . .

Anonymous eyewitness account of rioting over salt rights in El Paso, printed in the *Mesilla Independent*, January 7, 1878

THE LURE OF TEXAS

I said to Uncle Dick, who was born in Alabama, "You have really seen Texas change from 1839 until now [1929]."

"Yes, I have," he said. "I have been out here ninety years. I have begun to like it pretty well and have just about decided to stay and not go back to Tuscumbia."

Justin Van Gordon Anderson, *Recollections and Reflections of a Texian*, 1966

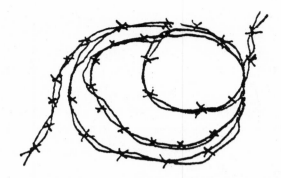

THE MACHINE THAT DID IN THE COWBOYS

When I saw a barbed-wire machine at work manufacturing it and was told that there were thousands of them at the same work, I went home and told the boys they might just as well put up their cutters and quit splitting rails and use barbed wire instead. I was just as confident then as I am today that wire would win. . .and that between barbed wire and railroads the cowboys' days were numbered.

W.S. James, *Cowboy Life in Texas*, 1893

★ ★ ★ ★ ★ ★ ★ ★ ★ ★ ★ ★ ★ ★ ★ ★

If we are to believe many of the writers of the day, murderers are to be met at every town, life is not safe for a moment, and private property is never respected. The whole of the population are described as dishonest and bloodthirsty; the very refuse of the vile. Texans are said to carry their national weapon, the Bowie knife, about them, and this alone, one would imagine, would lead to a frequency of assassinations.

Matilda Houstoun, *Texas and the Gulf of Mexico*, 1844

TEXAS POETICAL

Cautious words written into the state constitution at the time of Texas' entry into the Union provided for a contingent division of the state into five separate political units. When Lizzie Hamlett heard of the politics being played, she expressed the sentiments of every Texan in typical Big Country verse:

Divide the State! Who dare suggest
Such acts of sacrilege?
Who from us thus would basely wrest
Our holiest heritage?
Bought with a price, it is our own!
And shall we rend it twain
Which was cemented into one
by blood of heroes slain?

Divide the State! How then appease
The blessed name of those
Who watch with ceaseless jealousies
Their ashes' long repose?
Say for which portion Crockett fought?
For which did Travis die?
For which hath Houston's pleading bought
A nation's sympathy?
Say which shall claim Jacinto's plain,
Which own the Alamo?

Donald Day, *Big Country: Texas*, 1947

★ ★

Armadillo Eggs

1 pound monterey Jack cheese, grated and divided

1/2 pound hot pork sausage

1 1/2 cups buttermilk biscuit mix

1 package Shake 'n Bake mix for pork

15 small to medium canned jalapeno peppers

2 eggs, beaten

Slit and seed peppers. Stuff peppers with half the cheese and pinch peppers closed around the cheese. Mix remaining cheese and sausage. Add dry biscuit mix, one-third at a time, to make a stiff dough. Knead several times. Pinch off a bit of dough and pat into a flat pancake about 1/2 inch thick. Place a stuffed pepper in the middle of each pancake and wrap completely with dough, making sure that all edges and ends are sealed. Roll the dough-covered pepper in your hands to mold into an egg shape. Roll in Shake 'n Bake until coated. Dip in beaten eggs and roll again in Shake 'n Bake. Bake at 300 degrees for 20 to 25 minutes.

Attributed to Vanita Hull of Mansfield, collected by Bob Phillips in *Texas Country Reporter Cookbook*, 1990

TEXAS: A HAVEN FOR HENPECKED HUSBANDS

A husband expressed his domestic unhappiness to a judge. His wife was addicted to the bottle. The judge said:

"Lock it away from her."

"She's got all the keys"

"Don't let her have any money."

"She keeps all the cash."

"Well, then," said the judge, "part from her."

"She won't let me."

"Then I don't know what to advise. There's only one course—run off to Texas, for that is the land of promise for every rogue, fool, and discontented person here."

The Old American Comic Almanac, 1843

★ ★ ★ ★ ★ ★ ★ ★ ★ ★ ★ ★ ★ ★ ★ ★

WOMANLESS HOUSTON

"I am dying fast. The city is a desert. No business, no amusements. I have seen but one handsome woman here, and she wasn't pretty. I wish I could get a wife; try for me, do—will allow you a commission. I haven't a single button on all my shirts; plague on such a life, I say I must either marry or hang—no alternative."

letter to New England friend from bachelor in Houston, quoted in the *Houston Telegraph & Register*, December 19, 1838

COMIN' TO TEXAS BY SEA

The usual time for sailing from New Orleans to Texas was seven days, so we only took provisions for sixty persons for seven days, and about the time that was consumed our water also became alarmingly scarce—half a pint a day to each person. Being sick, I could not drink the water, nor the tea and coffee made from it. A little vinegar and sugar, diluted with this bad water, sustained me. . .

After our cooked provisions had given out, crackers and hard sea bread sustained life: but when the water gave out, then real suffering commenced. And such water! The well passengers could drink it made into coffee, but it so affected me that I could not endure the smell of coffee for several years. Mr. [?] Pilgrim says that he gave his share of the water to the children, and sustained himself on whiskey and crackers. . .

We had, a few days before, witnessed a burial at sea, and we naturally felt that unless relief came soon, it would be repeated. This was the first time I had ever experienced want—want of something to sustain life. . .so that when a hurricane drove us into Aransas Bay, no wonder we did not think of Indians. And now, again, as we enter Matagorda Pass, Sunday morning, January 27, 1829, with all our fears of hostile Indians, whose telegraphic smokes told of our approach, a joyful thankfulness filled our hearts, for we were entering the land of promise. . .

Mary Sherwood Wightman Helm, quoted by Jo Ella Powell in *Texas Tears and Texas Sunshine*, 1985

124

A GERMAN TRAVELER MEETS FRONTIER TEXAS METHODISTS

Mr. Huston, a true Methodist, informed me that divine service would be held in the schoolhouse, five miles away. . . . I rode with him to Squire Atkins, where we had dinner before hurrying to the meeting house. The Squire's daughter first intended to stay at home but let her father persuade her to ride along with us. All the people, men and women, ride on horseback to church here [in Texas].

About forty persons were assembled inside the log cabin, and some Negroes stood reverently on the porch. The singing started, and if I may say so, for those unending, bawling, nervewracking sounds contained nothing whatever that would have testified to any musical feeling. Thereafter Huston's young cousin reeled off a prayer, whereupon all of them fell on their knees, placed their heads between their hands into the pews and bellowed in long-stretched, gloomy tones: "God forgive us, we are all sinners, O Lord; O Lord, forgive us." Some became so enraptured that they helped complete the ceremony half-weeping, sighing and shouting.

[The parson] raged and blustered incessantly, declared all men, with the exception of the pious Methodists, to be sinners, and exhorted them to convert themselves, for not all of his listeners belonged to his sect. He walked about and pressed hands until three girls were so entranced they threw themselves upon the clergyman, began to cry, expressed their happiness as well as their sinfulness, and constantly urged us to become blessed otherwise. Squire's daughter succumbed to the unnatural excitement and fell to the ground unconscious. . . .

Some more times did the girls press our hands without success; the parson, amidst loud raging and many words, said nothing but that we were all sinners, and that the time had arrived for us to be come religious, that is to say, blessed, or Methodists. At length singing resounded in conclusion, and I felt quite blessed on being able to inhale the pure September air under God's free sky. I had often attended the service of Methodists, but this sensuous ecstasy, this abuse of the better feelings of man, aroused my indignation; I had never experienced anything like that.

Gustav Dresel, *Adventures in North America and Texas,* 1954

EARLY TEXAS WAS A DEBT-FREE SOCIETY, SORT OF

A high proportion of the early [Texas] settlers owed debts in the United States, which after 1829 were not collectible by suit until the defendant had been twelve years a resident. . . .[A] returned traveler said he was surrounded at every turn by the inhabitants of Texas, inquiring what he had done in the United States that had made it necessary for him to seek refuge in Texas. If one had run away from creditors only, he was regarded as a gentleman of the first water and welcomed on all hands, but if guilty of murder or high misdemeanor, they could assure him only of their protection.

Eugene Barker, *Quarterly of the Texas Historical Society,* 1919

PLAYPARTY ANTICS

Hope, Texas, and hundreds of other small rural communities. . . were blessed in frontier days with a form of entertainment called "playparties." These playparties were a type of dancing but could not be called that. Dancing was forbidden. Circuit-riding preachers condemned it as a sin, and the young people of these settlements were not allowed to go to the dance halls that were being operated in predominantly Catholic villages. Occasionally, Saturday night dances ended in drunken brawls, and this was condemned by the circuit-riding preachers also.

With no social life or entertainment on Saturday night the young people soon learned to meet at a neighbor's house and provide their own. Singing the songs they could remember was fine. This could include folk songs, or popular ballads, or even some songs that included square-dance calls. Some of these songs were not recalled accurately, but changing them or adding verses of their own was part of the fun.

After a few such sessions, groups began to think of "games" that could be used with some of the songs. These games were sometimes half-remembered dances. By singing certain songs and playing some of these games they could improvise movements or steps to go with them and have lots of fun singing and swinging. No one condemned them for this until instrumental music was added. The old folks drew the line there. When a fiddle and guitar were used, it was no longer a game; it was dancing and that was a sin.

To meet at a neighbor's house to sing and swing without instrumental music soon became acceptable. They were not dancing. They were singing and playing games, and finally this activity was given a name, a "playparty."

Kenneth Munson, quoted in *Texas Toys and Games,* 1989

★ ★

"A 'Texian,' as he calls himself, must not be expected to do much out of the saddle. When his feet leave his wooden stirrups, it is generally to tread the dance on the light fantastic toe. . . "

Mary Jaques, *Texas Ranch Life,* 1893

*N*ever shall I forget that trip to Laredo. . .

for I suffered much on it, physically and mentally. The weather was very trying for one so new to the country as I. The days were extremely warm and the nights uncomfortably cool. During the day the sun blazed in the heavens and the rays beat down on our heads with tropical force, but no sooner did the shades of night come on than the air grew icy cold, and before morning it was freezing. Two hours after the sun arose the next day, the terrible heat began again. To add to the discomfort of these extreme changes in temperature, water was very scarce and rattlesnakes extremely plentiful.

It was on this journey that I first experienced a Texas 'norther.' It came upon us early one afternoon. Will Ross and I were riding about a mile ahead of the wagon. We were coatless, and our shirts were open at the throats, for the heat was stifling. Suddenly, without the slightest warning, an icy wind swept across the prairie from the north. It chilled us, through and through, in a few seconds.

'Hello! A norther's coming,' said Will Ross. 'We'd better go back and get our coats.'

We turned back to the wagon, but when we attempted to ride in the teeth of that terribly cold wind, we suffered so that we gave up the attempt. We dismounted and stood in the lee of our horses until the wagon came lumbering up. Then we bundled into our coats and overcoats and rode on to a creek, a mile or so ahead. There, under the shelter of one of the banks, we built a great fire and went into camp, to remain until the 'norther' should blow itself out. This, Ross knew from experience, would be in two days.

A 'norther' invariably blows from the north for twenty-four hours. Then it comes back, almost as cold, from the south for twenty-four hours more. The third day there is no wind, but the cold continues, gradually abating until, on the fourth day, the temperature is what it was before the 'norther' came. I have been in New Hampshire when the thermometer marked forty degrees below zero; I have passed a night, lost in a snowstorm, in the Rocky Mountains in Colorado; but never have I suffered so from the cold as I have in a Texas 'norther.'

N.A. Jennings, *A Texas Ranger,* 1899

★ ★ ★ ★ ★ ★ ★ ★ ★ ★ ★ ★ ★ ★ ★ ★ ★ ★

Hail Facts

1. Some of the largest hailstones in Texas history fell in San Antonio in May of 1946. Many larger than Texas grapefruit struck the ground with such force as to bounce upward breaking second story windows.

2. Between 8:30 p.m. and 8:45 p.m. on the first day of March, 1973, a hailstorm struck Conroe, Texas, just north of Houston, covering Interstate 45 with hailstones 6 to 24 inches deep.

Harold Taft, *Texas Weather,* 1975

SWAPPIN' GUM IN EARLY TEXAS

Everyone has a passion for chewing gum. The ostensible reason for the habit is its tendency to increase the natural flow of saliva, and thus to remedy indigestion. The gum is aromatic and not unpleasant to chew, though the practiced chewer does not care for it in its original state; not, in fact, until he has rolled it in his mouth into a large insipid ball, resembling a lump of putty.

I have constantly found one of these balls of partially-chewed gum between the joints of a rocker (chair), left there in this delectable form in readiness for future enjoyment.

Happening to pay a visit on one occasion, I received a great compliment; nothing less than the offer of a piece of gum direct from the manipulator's mouth, after she had taken all the trouble to make it "just nice" for me. I was assured that it had come all the way from Virginia, and was "real good." It was no easy task to escape the ordeal of placing it in my own mouth on the spot, and finding the most ingenious excuses unavailing to avert the immediate reception of this fine (and perfected) Virginian gum, I thought that discretion was the better part of valour, and beat a hasty retreat.

The girls are great cigarette smokers, and many of them use the "dipping stick," although they refuse to own it. The matrons, however, make no secret of this nasty and offensive habit.

For the fun of the thing, I once asked a lady what she was doing, though I confess I was perfectly well aware of her weakness. She replied without hesitation:

"Cleaning my teeth, ma'am."

It certainly looked like it, as the tobacco juice oozed from her lips, to be squirted the next moment with perfect precision into the opening of the stove; a feat requiring infinite practice! "Dipping" is a kind of snuff-taking; the powder, which is a preparation of tobacco, being rubbed on the teeth and entirely over the gums with a piece of stick whittled at one end until it serves as a brush. The stick is almost always a root of the mesquite.

In order to make myself sociable I soon managed to take part in the cigarette smoking, and indeed, on subsequent occasions, when camping out, or during a long day's hunting, or on encountering bad smells in Mexican towns, I found the practice very useful.

Mary Jaques, *Texas Ranch Life*, 1893

★ ★ ★ ★ ★ ★ ★ ★ ★ ★ ★ ★ ★ ★ ★ ★ ★ ★

"**D**is yer's a quar country, stranger, you bet! All sorts of quar things out yer. Folks chop wood with a sledge-hammer and mow grass with a hoe. Every bush bears a thorn and every insect has a sting. The trees is pretty nigh all cactuses. The streams hain't no water, except big freshets. The rivers get littler, the furder they run down. No game but rabbits, and them's big as jackasses. Some quails, but all top-knotted, and wild as jackasses. No frost, no dew. Nobody kums here, unless he's runnin away. Nobody stays, unless he has to."

James Rusling, quoted in
A Treasury of Western Folklore,
edited by B.B. Botkin, 1975

128

GETTIN' TO TEXAS WAS NOT HALF THE FUN

Nightfall and a drizzling rain drove an elderly horseman traveling a road to Vicksburg to seek shelter near a roadside fire. As he approached, he saw around it the encampment of a family "amoving" to Texas, a very common sight in Mississippi in the year 1841. Two bodies wrapped in blankets lay close to the blaze. Near them a tow-headed boy, crying loudly, leaned against a front wheel of the wagon.

The horseman rode up and addressed him in a mollifying voice, "What's the matter, son?"

"Matter!" roared the piney-woods lad. "Fire and damnation, stranger! Don't you see mammy there shaking with ager [fever]! Daddy's gone afishing. Jim's got every cent of money there is, playing poker at a bit ante. Bob Stokes is gone on ahead with Nace! Sal's so corned she don't know that stick of wood from seven dollars and a half! Every one of the horses is loose! There's no meal in the wagon! The skillet's broke! The baby's in a bad fix, and it's a half mile to the creek. I don't care a damn if I never seen Texas!

Printed in the *Weekly Picayune* of New Orleans, 1841, as a comic illustration of hardships experienced when immigrating to Texas, quoted by Curtis Bishop, *Lots of Land*, 1949

TEXANESE

LICK

Molasses: Heavy, thick, strong-tasting, black syrup. A staple food of frontier Texas served at all meals and poured on almost all kinds of foods, from cornbread to pork chops.

The Texas 'Puncher' wasn't so much for pretty. . . Chances were he was dodgin' some sheriff and avoided sun-reflectin' gadgets like he would a swamp. But he had his vanity, too. His weakness was five pointed stars stitched to his boots, chaps, and saddle. For a Texan not to be totin' stars on his duds was considered most as bad as votin' the Republican ticket.

Ramon F. Adams, *The Old Time Cowhand*, 1948

THREE REASONS WHY EAST TEXAS IS DRAWKCAB

1. Remlig. Community founded in 1904 around sawmill operations in Jasper County. Peak population of 900. Sawmill closed in 1925. Town was backward spelling of founder Alexander Gilmer's last name.

2. Sacul. Farming community in Nacogdoches County. Population of 275 in 1940. Town was backward spelling of founding Lucas family.

3. Tinrag. Rural community of Hopkins County. Town was backward spelling of founding Garnit family.

Extracted from *The Handbook of Texas*, Vol. II, 1952

★ ★ ★ ★ ★ ★ ★ ★ ★ ★ ★ ★ ★ ★ ★ ★

"Me and Red Wing not afraid to go to hell together. Captain Jack heap brave; not afraid to go to hell by himself."

Said of Texas Ranger Captain John C. Hays, attributed to Flacco, a Lipan Indian, circa 1840

THE KILLING OF BIRD TRACY

Bird Tracy was mean.

He'd just as soon kill anybody for anything, 'specially if they made him mad. He killed two men round here [Hood County]. One of them was old Dan J. W. Parker. Tracy knew Parker had sold some cattle a few days before the murder and robbery occurred, and he knew the old man never put his money in a bank, so him and two of his cronies watched their chance and waylaid the old man and killed and robbed him. They must have got ten or twelve thousand dollars off him.

Old man Parker was a peculiar old cuss. He wouldn't have anything to do with anybody unless he knew them pretty well, and if you were talking to him and he saw somebody coming up to you that he didn't know he'd leave right now. He always wore an old coonskin cap and a deerhide coat and a pair of old duckin' pants with every color patch on it you could imagine. He was a scary looking thing to see coming out of the brush. He rode on one of the prettiest horses I ever saw, and I have never seen one like it before or since. It was golden in color with white spots on it.

Bird Tracy was nearly always in some kind of trouble round here. For months at a time he wouldn't come into town here because of some meanness he'd been in. If you met him he'd pull his hat down over his face to try to keep you from recognizing him.

His brother and I had a shooting scrape here on the courthouse square one time, and Bird talked around about how he was going to take the matter up with me, but he left here before he did anything about it, and he was killed while he was away. I guess if he had come back he'd have killed me, or I would have had to kill him.

He was in Shreveport, Louisiana, when Sid Carver killed him [about 1900]. Sid didn't live here in Granbury, but he would come in here to buy mules and horses, and Bird had helped him make some deals. So when Bird went to Shreveport he told Carver him and a saloonkeeper there could sell a couple of cars of mules for him. So Carver sent the mules, and Tracy and the saloon man billed the two cars of mules to some other place than the one Carver thought they were going to, and Bird and the saloon man, I don't know his name, sold the mules and beat Carver out of the money.

Carver went down there and run an attachment on the saloon and took charge of it. Tracy telephoned Carver he was coming to see him the next morning early at the saloon. Carver told him to come ahead. Carver got there about 6 o'clock and opened the saloon. Tracy came in a little while later, and started talking smart. Carver upped with his six-shooter and shot Tracy between the eyes.

Carver was a good man, and it seems he was also a good shot.

Library of Congress, WPA Federal Writers Project Collection; interview with Tom Mullins, Granbury, Texas, undated but circa 1935

"The Colorado [River] is in the same virgin and primitive natural state as the Congo in Africa, the Amazon in the Brazilian jungle, or the Ob and Jenisel in the wilds of Siberia."

Abraham Streiff, designer of Buchanan Dam, August 23, 1938, letter

I am a Texas Cowboy

I am a Texas cowboy
  lighthearted, gay and free,
To roam the wide, wide prairie
  is always joy to me.

My trusty little pony
  Is my companion true;
O'er plain, through woods and river
  He's sure to 'pull me through.'

I am a jolly cowboy,
  From Texas now I hail;
Give me my 'quirt' and pony,
  I'm ready for the trail.
I love the rolling prairie
  We're free from care and strife
Behind a herd of 'longhorns'
  I'll journey all my life.

The early dawn is breaking,
  Up, Up! we must away,
We vault into our saddles,
  And 'round up' then all day;
We 'rope' and 'brand' and 'ear mark'
  I tell you we are 'smart';
We get the herd all ready,
  For Kansas then we start.

And when in Kansas City,
  The 'Boss' he pays us up,
We loaf around a few days,
  Then have a parting cup;
We bid farewell to city,
  From noisy marts we come
Right back to dear old Texas,
  The cowboy's native home.

Author unknown,
traditional

GOD MISSED THE BOAT TO TEXAS

". . .[A] man rode up on the Louisiana side [of the Sabine River], evidently under great excitement, and at the top of his voice ordered the ferryman to bring over the boat. Supposing there was some emergency, the boat as promptly carried to the opposite shore, and the man landed as quick as possible on the Texas side.

"Just as he was ashore, an officer, with a body of men in pursuit of this refugee from justice, hailed on the eastern bank. The man, recognizing his pursuers, mounted his horse, rode up the hill entirely out of reach, and very deliberately made this short and pointed speech: 'Gentlemen, I am just a little too fast for your sort. You have no authority out of the United States. I am entirely safe.' Alighting from his horse and kissing the ground, he continued: 'The Sabine River is a greater Saviour than Jesus Christ. He only saves men when they die from going to hell; but this river saves living men from prison.'"

Zachariah Nehemiah Morrell,
Flowers and Fruits from the Wilderness, 1872

TEXAS LOST ★ ★ ★ ★ ★ ★ ★
Flomot, Texas

If you live in a Motley County ranching community very near the Floyd County line and a name is needed, what you do is name the town with the first three letters of each county and create a word. So, Flomot lives on FM 97 in northwestern Motley County—but very close to Floyd County.

It had a thousand verses
to it —the more whiskey,
the more verses.

Traditionally said of the classic
Longhorn herding song,
"The Chisholm Trail"

Black-Eyed Peas, Corn Bread, Tomatoes, and Onions

"When I was growing up on our Little River Stock Farm in central Texas in the 1930s (says Marion Travis), a smart alecky cousin from Dallas told me, 'Northerners don't eat black-eyed peas. They call them cow feed.'"

I was incredulous. Fresh black-eyed peas, with hot corn bread, fresh garden tomatoes and fresh onions were among my favorite foods—in the same class with my Grandmother Brewer's crisply fried chicken and Blue Bird vanilla ice cream from the Palace of Sweets in Cameron.

Properly selected, prepared and served they are an uninterrupted joy—the kind that clings in memory from Texan childhood throughout adulthood.

. . .Fresh black-eyed peas. They will popedy-pop-pop from their long greenish-purple pods into the pan in your lap as you shell them. Each pea is plump and a delicate green with a purplish-black eye. Snap a few young pods into the shelled peas. If you pick them yourself, a full-packed gallon bucket (in the hull) will serve four.

- 1 quart fresh shelled black-eyed peas
- 1 teaspoon salt
- 1 tablespoon fresh bacon drippings or two slices of uncooked, cured bacon
- Pan of hot corn bread
- 4 large, firm, ripe tomatoes
- 4 onions, approximately 1-inch in diameter
- Salt and pepper to taste

Wash shelled peas thoroughly in a colander or a pan. There will be some delicate pea skins remaining, which is good. Pour all into a large saucepan and cover with water. This becomes the pot liquor. Add salt and ease in fresh bacon drippings or bacon. Do not use margarine, butter, salt pork, ham or other oily ingredients. Cook on high heat until they reach a rolling boil. Turn the heat down to a slow boil for 20 minutes or until tender. The pot liquor will be dark. The peas will be darkish green.

While the peas are cooking, make your best recipe of corn bread. Perfect this in advance. Good corn bread is essential to the quality of the meal.

Slice tomatoes on a plate with onions. The onions should have green tops but do not have to be the tiny, mild onions often used in salads.

The layered feast should be arranged as follows: mound several spoonfuls of hot black-eyed peas into the center of your plate. Take a large piece of warm corn bread and crumble it quickly over the peas. It should have its stove heat when you begin eating. Do not butter your corn bread. Place cool tomato slices to taste on top of the corn bread and slices of crisp, cool onion to taste on top of tomatoes. Immediately ladle out several spoonfuls of warm pot liquor onto the plate. Not too many. You are not making soup, just a good eating consistency. Take knife in one hand, fork in the other and cut—over and over. This cuts up the tomatoes and onions, completes the corn bread crumbling and mixes the whole culinary marvel together. Dissimilarity in food textures, vegetable and bread temperatures and flavors makes this combination surpassingly delicious.

From *The Melting Pot: Ethnic Cuisine in Texas*, published by The Institute of Texan Cultures, San Antonio, 1977

A TEXAN EXPLAINS OKLAHOMA

Oklahomans are a fine, wonderful people given, like Texans, to chastising the infidel and fighting over governors. Texans and Oklahomans have fought, bled, and died together even when there was nobody else to fight. Even if this were not true, a Texan would have to be on Oklahoma's side. If there were no Oklahoma, there would be nothing on the north of Texas, and it is unthinkable for Texas to have a side on which it has nothing to be better than. Oklahoma serves a function. Texas is gigantic, of course, but it has to stop somewhere, and stopping short of Oklahoma is about right.

Oklahomans do not understand this. When the Department of Commerce published a booklet called "General Characteristics, Oklahoma," somebody remarked that it was a waste of the tax-payer's money. Everybody already knew the characteristics of Oklahoma—size, speed, deception, good blocking, and so on.

Paul Crume, *A Texan at Bay*, 1961

★ ★ ★ ★ ★ ★ ★ ★ ★ ★ ★ ★ ★ ★ ★ ★

TOUGH TEACHER

Out in Mason County, Texas, the first schoolmarm was an "Irish woman who had the strength of a strong man and the typical fighting spirit of her race. She kept a quart of whiskey and a leather quirt in her desk. The whiskey was strictly for her own use, the quirt for use on the kids."

Roy Holt, "The Pioneer Teacher," *Sheep and Goat Rancher*, Vol. XXXVI

NAMES OF TEN WILD HORSES RIDDEN BY TOM (BOOGER RED) PRIVETT, LEGENDARY TEXAS BRONCBUSTER

Montana Gyp
Flaxy
Moon
Texas Boy
Rocky Mountain Steve
Black Diamond
Gray Wolf
Hell to Set
Salty Dog
Bald Hornet

San Angelo Morning Times, April 25, 1933

A FAMILY TRAGEDY

Jim Swofford, living near Springtown in Parker county, attempted to chastise his son about a pistol one day last week and was resisted. He struck the son several blows with a chair, when the latter drew a knife and stabbed him near the heart, inflicting a wound which it is thought will prove fatal. The son escaped, and has not yet been captured.

Runnels County Record, January 26, 1884

Lima Bean Casserole

This unusual blend of flavors makes a savory casserole to be enjoyed as a side dish with barbecue or other meats or as a main dish itself.

1 pound dried lima beans

1 pound pork sausage, cut into cubes

2 green bell peppers, chopped

4 cups tomato sauce

2 cups milk

1 cup sour cream

2 tablespoons molasses

Wash beans. Cover with water and let soak overnight. Beans will double in bulk. Drain the beans and place in a 9-by-13-inch baking dish. Add cubed sausage and chopped peppers. Mix tomato sauce, milk, sour cream, and molasses together and add to beans. Mix well and cover pan with foil.

Bake at 325 degrees for 2 hours or until beans are done and most of the moisture is absorbed. Stir occasionally and add water if needed.

Candy Wagner & Sandra Marquez,
Cooking Texas Style, 1983

I left McNary county, Tennessee [1857], in a wagon drawn by three mules and a horse bound for Kerr county, Texas. In the wagon was packed our household goods, personal effects and enough food to last us two months. We averaged about 18 miles per day, and it took us 50 days to make the trip. Near San Antonio we met a young man on horseback who stopped us and asked us where we were going, and we told him "Kerr County." He said we would never be able to keep our mules and horse and that we had better turn back. After much deliberation we turned around and headed for DeWitt county, going by way of Gonzales, and stopped at the little settlement of Clinton, just across the river from the present town of Cuero, where we remained one year and rented land from Sam Calhoun. We planted 60 acres of corn and harvested 60 acres of nubbins [stunted corn ears]. We were so discouraged we decided to go to Kerr county and brave the depredations of the Indians. This we did, going immediately to a log cabin on the Watson Crook Survey, six miles southeast of Kerrville. This tract consisted of 640 acres, fronting one mile on the Guadalupe river and extending one mile to Turtle Creek, one-half of this tract being my present homesite on which I have lived for the past 54 years.

David Wharton, age 91, remembering his life in Texas,
Kerrville Times, April 1937

A SHORT DISCOURSE ON INDIAN SLEEPING HABITS

Most folks imagine the Indians just threw a pile of dirty skins down and burrowed into them. That isn't right. Four poles were fastened together with buffalo sinews, the end poles were pretty heavy and held the frame, about the size of our beds, off the ground. A dried buffalo hide was stretched tight and laced over the frame. That made pretty good springs. Buffalo robes were then spread over the frame with some on top for covers. I've slept in lots worse beds in white folk's houses many times.

Dot Babb, cowboy and onetime Indian captive,
interviewed for the *Amarillo Daily News,* August 11, 1936

DUCK FEATHERS AND JUNE BUGS

We had many struggles in the newspaper game, there in those early days. I remember a man from Robertson Peak paying his subscription with a bag of duckfeathers. My father sent me home with them in a howling norther and the string slipped off the mouth of the bag and the last I saw of them they were flying over the hill towards Ben Pittman's.

It seems strange what changes have taken place since that day away back there in 1882 when the first copy of *The Voice* went out. Coleman was small then; it didn't have a water or a lighting system until years later. It didn't even have telephones. The first telephone there was in *The Voice* office and the first conversation over a telephone I ever heard was between Rich Coffey and the operator at Baird. Uncle Rich said, "Get that d__d June Bug out of the box and talk to me."

Austin Callan, *Coleman Democratic-Voice*,
September 5, 1927

★ ★ ★ ★ ★ ★ ★ ★ ★ ★ ★ ★ ★ ★ ★ ★ ★ ★

AGGIE HORSES

"You know what this is?" [J.R. Robinson] asked, as he saddled the 16-hand, 1,250 pound Appaloosa gelding. "This here's a B.D.A.—Big Dumb Appaloosa. You know what they say about Appaloosas? 'No tail, no mane, no brain.' You know why the war chiefs made braves ride Appaloosas? 'Cause them dumb horses would make the Indians so mad they'd fight anybody."

Tom Bryant & Joel Berstein,
A Taste of Ranching, 1993

The Bluebonnets of Texas

It blooms upon our prairies wide
*   And smiles within our valleys*
A Texas flower, and Texas pride,
*   Around it honor rallies;*
And every heart beneath the blue
*   Transparent sky above it*
In Texaswise, forever true,
*   Shall fold, and hold, and love it.*

It blossoms free in homes and fields,
*   Made by love's labor royal;*
To fleur de lys or rose none yields
*   Allegiance more loyal!*
And to the world its flame shall go,
*   And tell the Lone Star's splendor*
Of hearths and homes that gleam
*   and glow*
*   Of loving hearts and tender.*

'Tis Texan in its beauty rare,
*   To honest hearts and appealing;*
And can there be a fame more fair,
*   Or deeper depth of feeling?*
For Texan hearts, in Texanwise
*   Are true to the Bluebonnet,*
And love it, as the bright blue skies,
*   That pour the blessings on it.*

John Sjolander, printed in *Here Is Texas*, 1936

The Comanches are a noble race of Indians . . . inhabiting the country to the north and northwest of San Antonio de Bexar. They are a wandering race, do not cultivate the earth for corn, but depend altogether upon the chase for subsistence. They follow the immense herds of buffaloe which graze the vast plains of this region, often to the amount of thousands in one herd. These plains are also stocked with wild horses, which run together in droves of many hundreds. These wild horses are called in the language of the country, Mustangs, and hence the figure of speech to denote any thing wild and uncultivated, as a mustang girl, applied to a rude hunter's daughter. These horses are not natives, but descended from the stock brought over by the first Spaniards. Domestic animals, and man himself, become rude, when removed from the associations of civilized life. The Comanches catch and tame these wild horses, and when unsuccessful in the chase, subsist upon them.

These Indians always move on horseback. Besides the bow and arrow, the usual arms of the Indian warrior, they are armed with a long spear, having a sword blade at the point. A war party of these mounted Indians is sufficiently formidable. They are headed by two squaws, who by their shrill voices, serve as trumpeters, and have, like them, various tones, to denote the different evolutions and movements. When they descry an object of attack, or pursuit, they dart forward in a column, like lightning, towards it. At a suitable distance from their prey, they divide into two squadrons, one half taking to the right, the other to the left, and thus surround it.

Though fierce in war, they are civil in peace, and remarkable for their sense of justice. They call the people of the United States their friends, and give them protection, while they hate the Mexicans and murder them without mercy. . .This hatred is mutual, and fully reciprocated on the part of the Mexicans. Hence the origin of the epithet expressing odium, so general in all parts of Mexico. To denote the greatest degree of degradation, they call a person a Comanche.

Mary Austin Holley, in a letter from Texas, dated December 1831

TEXAS RANGERS AS RENAISSANCE MEN

The Comanche had his warrior brave; the Mexican his caballero, ranchero or vaquero. To meet these, the Texans created the ranger, who, since he was the latest comer, found it necessary to adapt his weapons, tactics and strategy to the conditions imposed by his enemies. Each group of fighters influenced the others; and each remained the true representative of the customs and ideals of his respective race—its symbol of fighting genius.

The Texas Ranger learned much from his enemies; and in order to win or even to survive, he combined the fighting qualities of the three races. He could ride like a Mexican, trail like an Indian, shoot like a Tennessean, and fight like a devil.

Walter Prescott Webb,
The Texas Rangers, 1935

THE TIDES OF DESTINY SWEPT AWAY INDIANS

Perhaps nothing more should be said about the near-extermination of Texas Indians. Certainly any interpretation of the events in this history runs the risk of biased rationalization, either in defense of the savage tribes, or of their Texas-American conquerors. But even at this risk, one comment cries out to be made. It is that the actions of cultural bodies, whether savage tribes or literate, civilized states, should not, cannot, be judged in terms of individual morality. Cultures are not and never have been 'moral' in their dealings and relations with one another. Their treatment of one another is and has been ultimately determined by their relative strengths and the nature of their cultures, not by whatever their internal ethical or moral institutions happen to be. . .To view the events of Texas history from any such moralistic, narrow standpoint, as most histories have done, is to miss the magnitude and meaning of what happened.

Briefly, the obliteration of Texas Indians was but a small part, a footnote really, to the nineteenth-century development and emergence of a new, and in technological terms, a tremendously powerful nation-state. Given the accelerating industrial revolution of the United States, its spurting population growth, and the vast empty spaces of the West, inhabited mostly by a few Stone Age tribes of Indians, the inevitability of what had to happen becomes clear.

The dynamism of a new America, then as now, swept up willy-nilly its inhabitants, white and Indian, as a spring torrent sweeps up leaves and twigs for a journey to an unknown fate.

William Wilmon Newcomb, Jr., *The Indians of Texas*, 1961

OK, WE'RE ONLY MOSTLY PREGNANT

There is existing in the minds of the people in many places, if not generally, at the North, a strong and bitter prejudice against Texas. . .Because it has been represented to be the resort of criminals, of insolvent and fraudulent debtors, of outlaws, and bad characters of every description. Now, it cannot be, by any reasonable man, believed that the majority of the people of Texas are of such a character. . . No, it is believed only that a large part of the people of Texas are of the character described. Well, admitting they are, should the entire population and country be then reviled?

Chester Newell,
History of the Revolution in Texas, 1838

139

A RANCH'S SUPPLY ORDER

BOUGHT OF H. HUMPHREY:
CHANNING, TEX. 4-20[18]92

1 ax & handle	$1.25
100 lb. flour	2.65
88 lb. bacon	7.92
2 cans B. Powder	2.50
25 LB coffee	5.62
20 lb apples	2.00
20 lb. beans	1.10
2 lb. pepper	.50
10 lb. grapes	.75
25 lb. sugar	1.38
90 lb. rope	13.50
6 boxes ax grease	.60
1 lantern	1.00
1 oil can	.50
1 gal oil	.30
1 bot lemon extract	.75
1 bot vanilla extract	1.00
1 doz boxes matches	.25
9 sks salt	.25
10 lb. lard	.95
12 bars soap	.50
1 kg pickles	2.75

$43.82

Spring cattle roundup supplies bought
by the XIT Ranch from the Panhandle store
of H. Humphrey

OLD TEXAS JOKE; VERY OLD

Three cowboys, one from Texas, one from New Mexico and one from Oklahoma, met one day and started bragging about how tough they were. Finally they put up a pot of money for the one who could show himself the toughest. Soon they came upon a den of skunks. They decided that the one who could stay in the den the longest would surely be the most rugged of the three. They drew lots and the one from Oklahoma had to go in first. He lasted three minutes before he came running out with tears streaming down his face. The one from New Mexico went second, and he lasted ten minutes. The Texan walked in next. He hadn't been in ten seconds when all the skunks came high-tailing it out, headed for the wide open spaces.

Traditional

★ ★ ★ ★ ★ ★ ★ ★ ★ ★ ★ ★ ★ ★ ★ ★

FIRST TEXANS ENJOYED FILLY MIGNON

They were compelled to obtain their corn overland, and with much trouble, from Sabine or Bexar [San Antonio]. For months they were totally destitute of bread. Sugar and coffee were luxuries enjoyed only in remembrance or anticipation. Their only dependence for meat was upon wild game. To range the country for buffaloes was dangerous on account of the Indians. The mustangs, or wild horses, fortunately, were abundant and fat, and it is estimated that over one hundred of them were eaten during the first two years of the colony.

Mary Austin Holley, describing the hardships of
Steven F. Austin's colony Texas settlers,
from her book, *Texas: Observations Historical,
Geographical, and Descriptive,* 1833

A GENERAL STORE REMEMBERED

Were you ever in one of those old country stores? Have you ever, as a boy, stood in the wide open door close by the cracker barrels and looked back at the long row of shelves that lined both sides of the establishment your mother and father and "folks" depended upon for their supply of necessities during the long winter and spring seasons while crops were being planted or "laid by"? If you have not, you have missed an important chapter out of the Book of Life.

One side of the store contained shelves loaded with great bolts of calico and domestic cloths of varied colors, patterns and shade; jin-cys [?], woolens and heaving "shirting"—the latter sometimes used for the long cotton sacks used by pickers in the fall of the year. Another grade was called "canvas." Then, back behind was a long counter, on which there were great piles, row after row and stack after stack, of "overalls" and "jumpers." The "jumper" was a cheap, ready-made garment, loose-fitting and comfortable, worn like a coat, which in warm weather took the place of all other clothing from the waist up. They were made of a large checked material, resembling somewhat the Scottish plaids, and when brand new made a boy feel all dressed up. They came in mighty handy on hot days when a fellow went with a crowd over on Pecan [Creek] to go in swimming, or to the "Big Blue Hole" down below the bridge. In another section of the store was the hardware and glass ware, kettles, pots, pans, dishes and other kitchen equipment, while the space on the other side was reserved for groceries, including great slabs of side meat, flour, sugar, coffee, teas and a few extracts. Some of the country merchants even carried small stocks of furniture.

Then out back of the store, proper, they had the coops for the chickens and turkeys that were brought in from the country, and piles of crates in which to pack the eggs and ship them. The country merchant sold practically everything the cross timber farmer needed and bought everything he raised, even to his cotton and corn.

Worth S. Ray, *Frontier Times*, March 1942

☙ TEXANESE ❧

Arkansas Wedding Cake

Plain old ordinary corn bread. In the early years, the state of Arkansas served as a place Texans could look down on, and an entire lexicon of insults was aimed at citizens and customs of the smaller, poorer state, i.e.. an "Arkansas racehorse" was a razorback hog, and "Arkansas lizards" were body lice.

TEXAS EATS

Pickled Peaches

4 pounds ripe peaches

1 pint cider vinegar

3 cups sugar

1/2 teaspoon ground cloves

1/2 teaspoon ground cinnamon

1/2 teaspoon ground ginger

Cut up 1 peach. In a large pot; mix the peach, the vinegar, sugar, and spices. Bring to a boil; boil for 30 minutes, and strain. Return the syrup to the pot. When the syrup is boiling, bring a pot of water to a boil and drop the whole peaches in for 1 minute. Remove and skin the peaches. Add the peaches to the strained syrup and boil them for 5 to 10 minutes, until you can just pierce them with a knife. Do not overcook the peaches.

Put the peaches into sterilized jars and pour the boiling syrup over them. Preserve according to proper canning methods. Yield: 3 quarts.

Larry Ross, *Nanny's Texas Table*, 1987

W**hat has been listed as one of the decisive battles in history...** for paving American expansion to the Pacific. . .lasted some eighteen minutes. Houston's report of the losses was as close to true as anyone knew:

"In the battle our loss was two killed and twenty-three wounded, six of them mortally. The enemy's loss was six hundred and thirty killed. . .prisoners seven hundred and thirty. . .Santa Anna. . .included in the number.

"Our success in action is conclusive proof of daring intrepidity and courage. . .Nor should we withhold the tribute of our grateful thanks from that Being who rules the destinies of nations."

Noah Smithwick had been delayed by flooded streams and, to his disgust, missed the fight. He did arrive at the battlefield, however, in time to observe "rifles broken off at the breech, the stocks besmeared with blood and brains. . .The dead Mexicans lay in piles, the survivors not even asking permission to bury them, thinking, perhaps, that, in return for the butchery they had practiced, they would soon be lying dead themselves." At least one Mexican prisoner held a different opinion. Colonel Don Pedro Delgado wrote of their confinement: "I will only say, to the everlasting shame of our conquerors, that they kept us starving, sleeping in the mud, & exposed to frequent & heavy showers. Still more intolerable was the stench arising from the corpses on the field of San Jacinto; which they had not the generosity to burn or bury, after the time-honored custom."

On their way home at last, the Rose family had to cross the grisly plain at San Jacinto, the most direct route having been destroyed with Vince's Bridge. It was April 26, two days before [daughter] Dilue's eleventh birthday. "We left the battle field late in the evening. We had to pass among the dead Mexicans, and father pulled one out of the road, so we could get by without driving over the body, since we could not go around it the prairie [being] very boggy. It was getting dark, and there were now twenty or thirty families with us. We were glad to leave the battle field, for it was a grewsome [sic] sight. We camped that night on the prairie, and could hear the wolves howl and bark as they devoured the dead."

James Haley, *Texas: An Album of History*, 1985

★ ★

" The Russians might attack Washington, but I'll be damned if they'd be insane enough to attack Texas."

Robert Kaufman, U.S. Navy, rear admiral, defending the government's attempt to place a kind of DEW line transmitting system in the state, 1975

ONE VIEW: THE 'WHY' OF OUR REVOLUTION

The Texas Revolution was neither the culmination of a deep-laid program of chicanery or greed, nor the glorious response of outraged freemen to calculated oppression of tyrants. . .On the one side was the Anglo-American immigrant, blunt, independent, efficient, a rebel against authority, a supreme individualist. On the other side was the Latin American master of the soil, sensitive, secretive, subtle and indirect in his ways, by training and temperament a worshiper of tradition and a creature of authority. With the political ascendancy of the two elements reversed, the situation would have held no threatening aspects, but with the Mexicans in the political saddle conflict was certain.

Eugene C. Barker, *Mexico and Texas, 1821-1835*, 1928

★ ★ ★ ★ ★ ★ ★ ★ ★ ★ ★ ★ ★ ★ ★ ★ ★ ★

"I'm a dead man, boys, but don't let the others know it; keep on fighting to the death."

Traditional last words of Richard Andrews, considered the first man to die in the Texas Revolution at the Battle of Mission Concepción outside San Antonio, October 28, 1835

★ ★ ★ ★ ★ ★ ★ ★ ★ ★ ★ ★ ★ ★ ★ ★ ★ ★

A FUTURE TEXAS PRESIDENT MEETS TWO HEROES:
NOT A GOOD START FOR THE REVOLUTION

I was introduced to [Jim] Bowie—he was dead drunk; to [Sam] Houston—his appearance was any thing but decent and respectable, and very much like that of a broken-down sot and debauchee. The first night after my arrival, I was kept awake nearly all night by a drunken carouse in the room over that in which I 'camped.' Dr. [Branch] Archer and Gen. Houston appeared to be the principal persons engaged in the orgie, to judge from the noise. . . The whole burden of the conversation, so far as it was, at times, intelligible, appeared to be abuse and denunciation of a man for whom I had the highest respect, Gen. Stephen F. Austin.

Anson Jones, in autobiographical material published 1859; he was remembering his first meeting with Bowie and Houston at San Felipe in 1835

DIPLOMATIC COQUETRY

"Supposing a charming lady has two suitors. One of them she is inclined to believe would make a better husband, but is a little slow to make interesting propositions. Do you think if she was a skillful practitioner in Cupid's court she would pretend that she loved the other 'feller' the best and be sure that her favorite would know it?

"If ladies are justified in making use of coquetry in securing their annexation to good and agreeable husbands, you must excuse me for making use of the same means to annex Texas to Uncle Sam."

Marquis James, *The Raven*, 1929;
Sam Houston is explaining why he is
courting England and France as
political allies for Texas

TEXAS LOST ★ ★ ★ ★ ★ ★ ★
Mud, Texas

This little community rose up in 1880 east of Austin from, possibly, the watery sloughs of the Colorado River near Hornsby Bend. We presume the few residents named their settlement for what nature gave them to work with. Whatever the reason, Mud came, and Mud went. This now-departed village should not be confused with the Brazos County crossroads town of Mudville, which certainly still exists near Texas A&M, but that's probably just coincidence.

DYING TO SEE YOU

A young fellow named George Clutch had alienated himself from his family with his wild, unpredictable ways. They actually ran him off from home. After several years working on ranches in the Greenbelt area of Texas, he had settled down and married a lovely girl, and soon they had a darling baby daughter. He wanted to share his new condition with his folks, but he got word they didn't even open his letters.

George finally hit upon a plan. He made a compact with the undertaker. He got the undertaker to send his parents a formal invitation to their son's funeral. His trick worked; in a few days his entire family—father, mother, brothers, and sister—dressed in mourners' black, got off the train in Childress.

A person can imagine their consternation when the first person to meet them was their son.

His father, realizing his ingenuity, burst into gales of laughter, embraced George, blessed the beautiful wife and daughter, and reestablished friendly relations with the George Clutch family.

John O. West, *Cowboy Folk Humor*, 1990

TEXAS POETICAL

"*Now I lay me down to sleep,
While over me the graybacks
     creep.
If I die before I wake,
I pray the Lord my soul to take.*"

Traditional cowboy's lament,
related by Jesse James Benton,
Cow By The Tail, 1943;
"graybacks" were lice.

A SOLO JOURNEY

There is the story of the little boy who asked his father, "What is a Texian?"

His father replied, "Son, the story goes way back. Nearly 400 years ago Europe went busted. Many of the better people with brighter minds and more ambition began to move out. A man by the name of Columbus took the lead.

"About 200 years ago the banks of the Atlantic Ocean and for some distance inland were covered with these intelligent, industrious Europeans. About 145 years ago some of the more adventurous of these came to Texas. Their descendants are Texians."

Recollections and Reflections of a Texian, Justin Van Gordon Anderson, 1966; J. Frank Dobie defined a "Texian" as one whose ancestors came to Texas during the colonial and revolutionary periods (1821-1836)

M'LORD & A TEXAN

A visiting [English] duke and a Texas cowboy met in a saloon in Dodge City, and the Englishman offered to buy the Texan a drink. When the duke reached in his pocket for money to pay the barkeep, he chanced to bring out an old English coin. He showed it proudly to the cowboy. "You see the head of His Majesty the King on this coin? He made my grandfather a lord."

The cowboy regarded the strange coin with interest, then reached into his pocket and brought out an Indian-head penny. "See the head of that Indian on this here penny? He made my grandpappy an angel."

Sam P. Ridings, *The Chisholm Trail*, 1936

Make Me a Cowboy Again for a Day

Backward, turn backward, oh time with
your wheels,
Aeroplanes, buses and automobiles;
Dress me once more in sombrero and flaps,
Boots, flannel shirt and slicker and chaps,
Put a six-shooter or two in my hand,
Show me a yearling to rope and to brand,
Out where the sagebrush is dusty and gray
Make me a cowboy again for a day.

Give me a bronco that knows how to dance,
Buckskin in color and wicked of glance,
New to the feeling of bridle and bits,
Give me a quirt that will sting when it hits;
Strap on the blanket behind in a roll,
Pass me the lariat that's dear to my soul,
Over the trail let me gallop away
Make me a cowboy again for a day.

Thunder of hoofs on the range as you ride,
Hissing of iron and sizzling of hide,
Bellows of cattle and snort of cayuse,
Longhorns from Texas as wild as the deuce,
Midnight stampedes and milling of herds,
Yells of the cowmen too angry for words,
Right in the thick of it all would I stay
Make me a cowboy again for a day.

Under the star-studded canopy vast,
Campfire and coffee and comfort at last,
Bacon that sizzles and crisps in the pan,
After the roundup, smells good to a man;
Stories of ranchers and rustlers retold,
Over the pipe as the embers grow cold,
Those are the times that old memories play
Make me a cowboy again for a day!

Author unknown, circa 1940s

THERE'S A LOT OF EGO IN THE EYES OF TEXAS

[T]here arose a Texan way of life that still exists, even in the face of all the mass promotion and standardization of machine civilization. Stamina, individualism, "go-ahead" initiative, pride in everything Texas—these were and still are, in varying degrees, among the ingredients of the Texas spirit. Bitter courage, wry or raucous laughter, and kindliness stood out amidst the drabness and coarseness of frontier life. An astonishing number of urbane and intelligent men found a satisfying freedom from compulsion.

Indeed, the Republic of Texas worked a curious alchemy with its citizenry, educated and untutored alike. It took the sons and daughters of Tennessee, the Carolinas, Georgia, Mississippi, New York, France, and Germany and set its own ineffaceable stamp on their souls. The same process is still working in Texas today.

William Hogan, *The Texas Republic*, 1946

★ ★ ★ ★ ★ ★ ★ ★ ★ ★ ★ ★ ★ ★ ★ ★

SALOON MENU

Rowdy Kate

Rag-Time Annie

Drowsy Dollie

Crippled Callie

Box-Car Jane

Panhandle Nan

Fickle Flossie

Old Ella

Midnight Rose

Nicknames of "Queens" and "Soiled Doves" working in Hog-Town, Tascosa's major saloon, about 1880

TEXANESE

Home-Sucker

A disparaging expression, usually spoken sarcastically by ranchers and cowboys, for farmers who plowed grassy grazing pastures into fields. Doubtless, the term came from "homesteader" or "homeseeker." Because of little rain in western Texas, it was believed that farming was a useless venture. Irrigation changed that opinion, but cattlemen always believed farming was a lesser occupation for a real man to take up.

Squat

A derivative of "squatter," meaning someone settles on land without legal title. In early Texas this word also was a noun. It meant a small parcel of land or a mineral claim, as in "He's got hisself a mean little squat of dirt." Sometimes such an unworthy piece of land was called a "go-broke farm" or a "starve-out ranch."

Texas' Jackass Mail Saves San Diego

We take great pleasure in announcing to our readers in the upper country, that the Overland Mails which left San Antonio on the 26th [July] under the contract entered into between the government and James F. Birch, Esq., of Sacramento, arrived on the 31st, at noon precisely, in charges of Mr. James E. Mason, the party. . .having made the trip in the unprecedentedly short time of 34 traveling days. . .

The event naturally created the greatest enthusiasm among our people, and was hailed with a salute of 100 anvils, the firing of crackers, and the general congratulations of the citizens. It was looked upon as the most important event which has ever occurred in the annals of San Diego.

San Diego Herald, September 5, 1857

TEXAS POETICAL

Hell's Half Acre

*On the south end of Fort Worth,
    between Jones and Main,
There was a small area of sin and
    shame,
Where many a good man, met his
    maker,
It was known far and wide as Hell's
    Half Acre.
It was a place for gamblin', women
    and fun,
And all of the cowboys carried a gun.
It was a place for outlaws, with a
    price on their head,
And many a man goin' there ended
    up dead.
It was a stoppin' place for cowboys on
    the Chisholm Trail.
They were lookin' for a good time,
    some ended up in jail.
It was a place where lawmen didn't
    want to be,
'Cause the outlaws would kill them
    just to be free.
The men who chased women were
    known as takers,
At least that's what they called them,
    down in the Acre.
And the women stood at the windows,
    wavin' to the men,
They wanted to party, drink with
    them and sin.
There wasn't any trouble, findin'
    women in these places.
You could tell by their clothes and the
    makeup on their faces.
It was easy to find, when you rode into
    town,
All you had to do was just to look
    around,
Knowin' that you could meet your
    maker,
'Cause you were in the middle of
    Hell's Half Acre.*

Bob Renshaw, *Fort Worth*, 1995

TEXAS IS.....

The "Old Man River" of states. No matter who runs it or what happens to it politically, it just keeps rolling along.

Will Rogers, circa 1930s

★ ★ ★ ★ ★ ★ ★ ★

A most delicious country; fertile, bountiful prairies covered with grass and flowers.

Senator Thomas Benton, circa 1829

★ ★ ★ ★ ★ ★ ★ ★

Cards and vulgar slang and stories of Indian adventures form the staple of [Texans'] mental exercises.

M.K. Kellog, *Texas Journal*, August 1872

COLLOQUIAL TEXAS

"Teneha, Timpson, Bobo and Blair" was the conductor's call along the small East Texas rail line in Shelby County. This lyrical quartet of consecutive small towns gave their names to a memorable line in a venerable country-western song, "Teneha, Timpson, Bobo and Blair, let me get off just any ole where." And, best of all, Texans who fought in World War I introduced others to the four towns as an urgent plea when craps shooting: "Teneha, Timpson, Bobo and Blair. . .Give me a seven, see if I care."

THE MESQUITE SCOURGE

The mesquite is an erratic tree. Instead of seeking the sky and competing with its neighbors for height, it crawls and wallows in the sand. Its trunk never grows straight up, nor does it limit itself to one trunk only. It may have several trunks, snaking along on the ground, suddenly leaping upward for a few feet only to duck down again or circle in another direction.

Unpredictable, extravagant in space and growth, unexplainable, it is like a snake in many ways. Its leaves are forked and thread-like as a serpent's tongue, with branching petals arranged like ladder rungs, reflecting sunlight in a bewildering variety of directions. The shade of green thus created is rich and delicate beyond that of any other foliage in the world. In the spring it is spangled with yellow blooms destined to mature into long bean pods.

Sometimes the mesquite is almost like a vine, so dependent does it seem on the ground for the support of its whole serpentine length. The trunk can support a vast spread of limbs because the wood is tough and strong; and, though flexible enough not to break under a strain, it is hard to bend at will. From a distance, the mesquite does not resemble a tree, but looks like a huge half-grove of green, bubbling out of the ground. Its most outspread branches usually scrape the sand.

Under, or rather inside, this living dome is a sort of cove where cattle can find protection not from the sun, for the foliage is too thin to keep out many rays, but from the rope, the dehorning tongs, the branding iron, and other human instruments of pain.

In the sandy land of the vast river bed between Norias and the Gulf coast, mesquites grow close together, sometimes no more than three feet apart, each shooting its harum-scarum branches into the midst of those of its neighbors. In places, they are impossible to get through on horseback. In the loam around Sauz, below the southern boundary of the sandy area, they also grow in abundance, providing a safe haven for the successors of the longhorn cattle that had originally brought them there.

Frank Goodwyn, *Life on the King Ranch,* 1951

"*Taffy does not grow on trees in Texas.*"

William Cowper Brann, *The Iconoclast,* 1896

A TEXAS RANGER PORTRAIT

The qualifications necessary in a genuine Ranger were not, in many respects, such as are required in the ordinary soldier. Discipline, in the common acceptation of the term, was not regarded as absolutely essential, a power of endurance that defied fatigue, and the faculty of "looking through the double sights of his rifle with a steady arm,"—these distinguished the Ranger, rather than any special knowledge of tactics. He was subjected to no "regulation uniform," though his usual habiliments were buckskin moccasins and overhauls, a roundabout and red shirt, a cap manufactured by his own hands from the skin of the coon or wildcat, two or three revolvers and a bowie knife in his belt, and a short rifle on his arm. In this guise, and well mounted, should he measure eighty miles between the rising and setting sun, and then, gathering his blanket around him, lie down to rest upon the prairie grass with his saddle for a pillow, it would not, at all, occur to him he had performed an extraordinary day's labor. The compensation received from government at that time was one dollar a day. . .

Nelson Lee, *Three Years Among the Comanches*, 1859

BLACK PETER MAKES HIS POINT

. . .[O]ne of the most ghoulish characters in Texas history [was] Black Peter. The huge Negro seemed immune to cholera and when he appeared to request employment as city undertaker [in Victoria, 1833], he was speedily appointed. His fee was $2.50 and a quart of whiskey for each body taken to the public graveyard. Each night and each morning Black Peter made his rounds, knocking at each door and shouting out the sickening cry to "bring out your dead." If there was no answer, Black Peter entered the house and conducted a thorough search. At the height of the epidemic the alcalde notified Black Peter that the town could no longer pay him. That night Peter made his rounds as usual collecting his corpses but, instead of carrying them to the city graveyard, deposited them all on the alcalde's front porch. Next morning the alcalde resumed payments. From Victoria, Black Peter went on to New Orleans to pursue his grim trade.

Curtis Bishop, *Lots of Land*, 1949

TEXAS POETICAL

Wind

*A stranger sat on the
    farmhouse porch,
And felt the dry wind
    sing and scorch;
It rustled the grain
    the old man had
    sowed;
It swirled the dust in
    the country road.
The stranger
    questioned of
    wind and grime,
If it blows like that for
    long at a time.*

*The old man scanned
    with faded eyes
The wind-swept plains
    and the moving skies.
With a gnarled brown
    hand he scraped
    his chin,
And made reply with
    a faded grin;
"It blows like this for
    months at a spell;
The rest of the time it
    blows like hell!"*

A.L. Crouch, printed in
Out Where the West Begins, 1949

149

COWBOYS AT PLAY

Talking about gambling and drinking makes me think how easy it can get men into trouble. While I was on the Slaughter Ranch a bunch of boys went to Big Springs to a picnic and got to drinking and having a general good time. The north part of town was the Mexican part. Those Mexicans had more dogs and more kinds of dogs than I ever saw. They had the first hairless dogs I ever saw. They had woolly dogs. You could hardly see their eyes. Of course they had the common old dog, the kind you see all over the country. In passing through town that whole bunch of dogs took after the boys. They could not stand for that and they went to shooting at the dogs and killed some of them and crippled some others. Of course the Mexicans did not like that. The Mexicans, some of them, came out with their guns but did not do any shooting. The boys. . .had all the fun they wanted, put spurs to their horses, and ran off. . . .

Some of the same boys moved their camp out near Stanton in Martin County. They got to drinking one day and shot up the town, as they called it—shot some chickens and dogs, shooting up in the air and having lots of fun. The citizens began to bunch up in the streets and looked as if they might interfere. The boys saw the people did not seem very well pleased with the way they were acting. They ran off as they did at Big Springs.

But there came a time when all of them did not run out of town, for the settlers got tired of such foolishness and shot back at them and killed one cowboy. They did not see why they should sit there and let a bunch of wild cowboys have so much fun at their expense. . .They killed John Dogie and shot a hole through Henry Mason's hat.

The bullets began to sing around the other boys' heads. They decided to get away and they did.

I thought it was just too bad that John had to get killed for he was as good a cow hand as there was on the Slaughter Ranch. . . He was kind-hearted and a good worker, always at his place when there was work to do. I think he was just about the best calf flanker I ever saw.

Rufe O'Keefe, *Cowboy Life*, 1936

WE TOLD YOU SO

"Cowboys can be divided into two classes: Those hailing from the Lone Star State, Texas, the other recruited from Eastern states. The Texans are unrivaled in horsemanship, hardihood and skill with rope and gun."

Baillie W. Grohman,
"Cattle Ranches in the Far West,"
article in undated issue of
Cornhill Magazine, circa 1885

A LITTLE SNEAKY, BUT IT WAS WAR

[D]ay revealed to us a regiment of [Mexican] lancers approaching us. . .they were after our blood. Our colonel [Jack Hays], seeing our situation, with some of the boys barely yet awake, tried to gain a little time to better prepare us to receive the charge. He rode out front with his saber in his hand and challenged the colonel of the lancers to meet him halfway between the lines to fight a saber fight.

Hays knew no more about saber fighting than I did. . . So, as soon as the Mexican colonel could divest himself of all encumbrances, he advanced waving his saber, while his horse seemed to dance rather than prance. Within a few feet of the Mexican, Hays pulled a pistol and shot him dead from his horse.

Buck Barry, A Texas Ranger and Frontiersman, 1932; Barry is recalling action by Texas Rangers at the Battle of Monterrey during the U.S. Mexican War

★ ★ ★ ★ ★ ★ ★ ★ ★ ★ ★ ★ ★ ★ ★ ★ ★

MURDER COLD AND BLOODY

Early last evening W.C. Frazier, alias "Bud," a worthless character living near Mason, shot and killed W.F. McNealy, head boss for Schreiner, Lytle & Light in this county. A long standing grudge against McNealy was the cause of the killing, which was a cold blooded murder, shooting him in the back. Frazier immediately mounted a horse and fled and still is at large with a party in pursuit. Nothing has been heard of him as yet. Great indignation is manifest and a reward of $500 is offered by the Light brothers.

Runnels County Record, November 8, 1884

"Corner Twelve, Rusk Street, Fort Worth, Texas"

Title of late 19th-century fiddle tune often heard in Hell's Half Acre, that city's red-light district

GREAT EXPECTORATIONS

The St. Leonard Hotel [in San Antonio] is much frequented by Texas ranchmen, some of whom are not very refined in their habits. On the staircase, at the time of my visit, a notice was displayed requesting, "Gentlemen not to spit on the floors, walls or ceilings;" and the request was by no means unnecessary.

Mary Jaques, Texas Ranch Life, 1894

TEXAS LOST ★ ★ ★ ★ ★ ★ ★ ★
Mukewater

In southeastern Coleman County, this community began in the 1860s as an early far western trading post, and was named for the poor grade of drinking water found there. Or, claims another source, it's the muddled name of a Comanche chief. Whatever, Bill Franks ran the store, and he was a practical joker, enjoying such gags as mousetraps in the cracker barrel and pepper in snuff bottles. Soon, people began calling the settlement "Trick'em," and that was the name submitted for a post office. Postal authorities, inexplicably, changed the name to Trickham, and Trickham it remains today.

★ ★ ★ ★ ★ ★ ★ ★ ★ ★ ★ ★ ★ ★ ★ ★ ★

"Have Faith in Texas"

Motto for state during long drought of 1950s

The Ol' Cow Hawss

When it comes to saddle hawsses,
There's a difference in steeds;
There is fancy-gaited critters
That'll suit some fellers' needs;
There is nags highbred and tony
With a smooth and shiny skin,
That will capture all the races
That you want to run them in.
But for one that never tires,
One that's faithful, tried and true;
One that allus is a 'stayer'
When you have to slam him
     through,
There is but one breed of critters
That I ever come across
That will allus stand the racket
It's the Ol' Cow Hawss.

No, he ain't much for beauty,
For he's scubby and he's rough,
And his temper's sort o' sassy
But you bet he's good enough.
'Cause he'll take the trail o'
     mornin'

Be it up or be it down,
On the range ahuntin' cattle
Or alopin' into town;
And he'll leave the miles behind
     him
And he'll never sweat a hair
'Cause he is a willin' critter
When he's goin' anywhere.
Oh, your thoroughbred at runnin'
In a race may be the boss,
But for all-day ridin'
Lemme have the Ol' Cow Hawss.

When my soul seeks peace and
     quiet
On the Home Ranch of the Blest,
When no storms nor stampedes
     bother
And the trails are trails of rest,
When my brand has been inspected
And pronounced to be O.K.
And the Boss has looked me over
And has told me I kin stay,
Oh, I'm hopin' when I'm lopin'
Off across that blessed range,
That it won't be in a saddle
On a critter new and strange!
But I'm prayin' every minute
That up there I'll ride across
That big heaven Range o' Glory
On an Ol' Cow Hawss.

E.A. Brininstool, about 1935

152

The Stampede

Lightin' rolls in hoops and circles,
Rain in sheets is comin' down,
Thunder rattles through the gulches,
As the hoofbeats shake the ground.

Top hands ride like likkered Injuns
Beggin' God for break o' day.
A stampede beats the best camp meetin'
When it comes to gettin' men to pray.

Walt Cousins, 1938

TEXANESE

Beef head

This was a term given Texas cowboys who drove cattle up the trail into Kansas. While not altogether uncomplimentary—it was more of a geographic identifier than a descriptive expression—the name generally carries a negative implication and, in certain environments (like a saloon), created social discord. "Aw, that ol' boy's a beef head," often produced splendid fistfights.

TEXAS EATS

Hilda's Cowboy Cooking Pinto Beans

2 cups dried pinto beans

1 tablespoon bacon grease

1 clove garlic, minced

1/2 cup chopped green chile

1/2 cup catsup

1 teaspoon Worcestershire sauce

Completely cover beans with water and soak at least overnight. (Soaking for 24 hours is better). Beans may be cooked in soaking water. Add the bacon fat to the water to keep from boiling over. Add the garlic and green chile peppers. Add the catsup and Worcestershire sauce. Cook with a tight lid (the tighter the better) and cook at least eight to 10 hours. Keep beans covered with water and add hot water if more is needed. Do not salt beans while they're cooking. (Salt seems to keep `em from cooking through.)

Tom Bryant and Joel Berstein,
A Taste of Ranching , 1993

Cream Gravy

1 tablespoon oil or fat

2 tablespoons flour

2/3 cup heavy cream

2/3 cup milk

1/2 cup chicken broth

Salt and pepper

Drain off all but 1 tablespoon oil or fat from a roasting or frying pan used to make. . .fried steak, fried chicken or any roasted bird. Stir in the flour until smooth. Add the cream, milk, chicken broth, and stir until smooth. Heat to the boil, stirring and scraping any bits off the pan bottom, and simmer for 5 minutes, until thickened and smooth. Season to taste with salt and pepper. Serve at once. Yield: 1 3/4 cups.

Jerry Flemmons, a long-time writer and editor for the *Fort Worth Star-Telegram*, is a columnist for the newspaper's "Weekly Review" section and Writer in Residence at Tarleton State University. He is author of six books and a play. ★